T0319101

Cambridge Elements ☰

Elements in Earth System Governance
edited by
Frank Biermann
Utrecht University
Aarti Gupta
Wageningen University

DECARBONISING ECONOMIES

Harriet Bulkeley
Durham University

Johannes Stripple
Lund University

Lars J. Nilsson
Lund University

Bregje van Veelen
Durham University

Agni Kalfagianni
Utrecht University

Fredric Bauer
Lund University

Mariësse van Sluisveld
Netherlands Environmental Assessment Agency

CAMBRIDGE
UNIVERSITY PRESS

CAMBRIDGE
UNIVERSITY PRESS

University Printing House, Cambridge CB2 8BS, United Kingdom

One Liberty Plaza, 20th Floor, New York, NY 10006, USA

477 Williamstown Road, Port Melbourne, VIC 3207, Australia

314–321, 3rd Floor, Plot 3, Splendor Forum, Jasola District Centre, New Delhi – 110025, India

103 Penang Road, #05–06/07, Visioncrest Commercial, Singapore 238467

Cambridge University Press is part of the University of Cambridge.

It furthers the University's mission by disseminating knowledge in the pursuit of education, learning, and research at the highest international levels of excellence.

www.cambridge.org
Information on this title: www.cambridge.org/9781108928748
DOI: 10.1017/9781108934039

First published 2022

A catalogue record for this publication is available from the British Library.

ISBN 978-1-108-92874-8 Paperback
ISSN 2631-7818 (online)
ISSN 2631-780X (print)

Cambridge University Press has no responsibility for the persistence or accuracy of URLs for external or third-party internet websites referred to in this publication and does not guarantee that any content on such websites is, or will remain, accurate or appropriate.

Decarbonising Economies

Elements in Earth System Governance

DOI: 10.1017/9781108934039
First published online: January 2022

Harriet Bulkeley
Durham University

Johannes Stripple
Lund University

Lars J. Nilsson
Lund University

Bregje van Veelen
Durham University

Agni Kalfagianni
Utrecht University

Fredric Bauer
Lund University

Mariësse van Sluisveld
Netherlands Environmental Assessment Agency

Author for correspondence: Lars J. Nilsson, lars_j.nilsson@miljo.lth.se

Abstract: Based on an interdisciplinary investigation of future visions, scenarios, and case studies of low-carbon innovation taking place across economic domains this Element, Decarbonising Economies, analyses the ways in which questions of agency, power, geography, and materiality shape the conditions of possibility for a low-carbon future. It explores how and why the challenge of changing our economies is variously ascribed to a lack of finance, technology, policy, and public engagement and shows how the realities constraining change are more fundamentally tied to the inertia of our existing high-carbon society and limited visions for what a future low-carbon world might become. By showcasing the first seeds of innovation seeking to enable transformative change, Decarbonising Economies will also chart a course for future research and policy action towards our climate goals. This Element is also available in the Open Access section on Cambridge Core.

Keywords: decarbonisation, low-carbon transition, net zero, energy-intensive industry, reducing consumption

ISBNs: 9781108928748 (PB), 9781108934039 (OC)
ISSNs: 2631-7818 (online), 2631-780X (print)

Contents

1 Introduction

All around the world – spurred on by the weight of scientific evidence, increasing vocal public protests, and shifting economic interests – governments are declaring ambitious goals for decarbonising the economy. If 30 years ago commitments to reduce greenhouse gas (GHG) emissions by 20 per cent appeared out of the ordinary, today's targets focus on the holy grail of achieving a *net-zero* economy where emissions are reduced and balanced by increasing the capacity for Earth's systems to absorb carbon. At the same time, our understanding of the climate problem has shifted. Rather than being a matter of emission reduction at the 'end of pipe' in the energy and transportation sectors, addressing climate change is now regarded as requiring the wholesale transition of the economy and the transformation of society. Climate change is no longer a stand-alone issue but a deeply embedded one in the workings of our political economies and everyday lives.

Yet, for all of the ambition expressed and the realisation that decarbonisation requires systemic change across the economy, attention remains trained on a few areas of carbon production and consumption – primarily electricity, heat, and transportation. Although vital for achieving the decarbonisation of economies, a focus on these areas of our economic and social life only provides a partial picture of the challenges and opportunities of decarbonisation. For a start, understanding the potential for transitions in electricity, heat, and transportation requires that we understand their embedded role in our wider economy – as the basis for a huge range of industrial processes, patterns of consumption, dynamics of urbanisation, and so forth. Equally, understanding how and by what means decarbonisation is emerging in a range of other sites and arenas of the economy which are carbon-intensive will also be critical to reaching net zero. In this Element, we bring these carbon-intensive areas of the economy into the spotlight. Focusing on parts of the economy that contribute significantly to the climate problem – steel, plastic, paper, meat, and milk – we explore how low-carbon futures are being envisioned, enacted, and contested in the European Union (EU) and what this means for the challenge of decarbonising economies.

While there is growing interest in how decarbonisation can take place across these areas of the economy amongst the public and the issues are increasingly making their way on to policy agendas across Europe, to date, they have received limited attention from the social sciences. While accounts of the challenges and possibilities of decarbonisation in each of these sectors individually are emerging, bringing analyses of these sectors together allows us to explore the different dilemmas they raise for decarbonisation and what this means for the governing of the Earth system in the decades ahead. Our account focuses on the European Union, where the underpinning research for this Element undertaken by the REINVENT project was conducted. As a region, the EU has some of the most ambitious plans for decarbonisation in the world, recently underpinned by the 2020 Green Deal. At the same time, the EU is of course no island, and the approaches taken to decarbonisation within the EU will both shape and be structured by how the global value chains that underpin the production of steel, plastic, paper, meat, and milk respond to the decarbonisation challenge. In the sections that follow, we take account of the political economies and geographies of decarbonisation in the EU, attending to the visions that are being articulated for how such sectors can reach net zero, the initiatives and innovations that are being developed to generate decarbonisation across the value chain from production to consumption, and the realities that these sectors face in confronting the decarbonisation challenge. First, in the rest of this section, we set out the challenges that decarbonisation entails when we start to move beyond the primary use of energy and consider the current and future contributions that carbon-intensive parts of the economy will need to make if we are to reach net zero.

Unmaking and Remaking Carbon Economies

That carbon and the fossil fuels and agricultural emissions through which it is produced are so central to modern economies is no accident. Carbon is a fundamental element of the socio-technical systems through which economies are organised and political societies and everyday practices are constituted (Mitchell 2011). Over the past two decades, a substantial body of evidence has been developed that suggests that socio-technical systems develop inherent inertia or 'lock-in' that serves to cement path dependence for high-carbon economies (Bernstein and Hoffmann 2018). This Element has pointed to the importance of both technical and social innovation in breaking through existing systems and institutions to generate low-carbon transitions, pointing to the critical importance of protecting and nurturing innovation niches. If early accounts of such transitions appeared to suggest that relatively linear transition pathways could be generated given the right external conditions and mix of (locally) powerful actors, more recent work suggests that such pathways are rarely so straightforward and that the structural, socio-material, and geographical configurations of existing regimes matter a great deal in terms of shaping the potential for decarbonisation (Geels 2019; Haarstad and Wanvik 2016; Stripple and Bulkeley 2019). There are, in short, political economies at work that serve to actively sustain the high-carbon economy. Understanding these dynamics – including the relation between state and capital, the structure of value chains, and flows of investment – will therefore be vital in establishing the opportunities and challenges for decarbonisation.

At the same time, it is vital that we recognise that high-carbon economies are not only a matter of politics and economy but also a matter of culture 'in its broad sense of the meanings that we give social life and material objects, and the concrete practices that they enable and depend on for their sustenance' (Best and Paterson 2009: 4). The everyday practices through which we use energy, organise our mobility, consume food, wear clothes, shop for household objects, operate our workplaces, and so forth all contribute to generating particular ideas and values about what constitutes the 'good life' and how it should be realised. For the vast majority, our cultural imaginations of the future and our lives within it are shaped by a desire for a good life fuelled by carbon. Decarbonisation, or put more simply the 'un-making' of carbon, is then not only a matter of socio-technical innovation or of changing the political-economic structures through which high-carbon economies are sustained but also a matter of understanding how our desires and identities are intimately bound up in the high-carbon economy and the ways in which these can be contested and reconfigured. It is thus also a question of making new economies and remaking those meanings and identities that align with pathways towards reaching climate neutrality by 2050. In this Element, we adopt this broadly cultural political economy per-spective to understand both the challenges and the opportunities for decarbon-ising economies.

The Scale of the Challenge

To get a sense of the decarbonization challenge it is worth noting that the greenhouse gas emissions from steel, plastics, paper, meat and milk are each similar in size to large country emitters such as Japan or Russia, as well as total EU27 emissions. For example steel, an important construction material with rapidly growing demand in developing countries, accounts for about 7 per cent of global carbon dioxide emissions. With an ever-growing world population and the rapid industrialisation of various emerging economies, the basic material industries look set to continue to be major contributors to global carbon emissions.

The current state-of-the-art knowledge on the mitigation efforts needed to stay in line with the Paris Climate Agreement (UNFCCC 2015) has underscored the need for major carbon emission reductions across carbon-intensive sectors of the economy. In order to limit global average temperatures to between 1.5 and 2 degrees centigrade compared to pre-industrial levels, a global coordinated effort by the full breadth of the industry to reduce carbon emissions by about 50–100 per cent in developed countries in 2050 will be required. Although some regional differences are accounted for in these estimations (see Figure 1), it is clear that there is limited leeway available for developed countries in addressing these targets compared to developing or emerging countries.

Imaginary Worlds

Responding to this challenge has required not only normative ambitions but also the means through which to make a leap of the imagination – to envisage a 'climate-neutral Europe by 2050' in which these sectors of the economy are fundamentally changed. To Wolf (2012: 17), such 'imaginary worlds' represent realms of possibility, a mix of the familiar and unfamiliar, of dread and dream, that can make us more aware of the circumstances of the actual world we inhabit. In the past 10–15 years, descriptions of the possibilities of a climate-neutral Europe by 2050 have emerged in the form of scenarios and visions. Various scientific methods have been developed over time to support decision-makers in composing such a perspective, ranging from qualitative to quantitative forward-looking methods (Elzen et al. 2004; Nilsson et al. 2008; Voinov and Bousquet 2010).

As a result, a wide range of decarbonisation visions exist, integrating knowledge from a local, regional, or (supra)national level. Figure 2 provides a snapshot of decarbonisation pathways considered for carbon-intensive sectors of the economy in Europe. These visions have looked at either the needed change in the sector to reach specific climate objectives or the technical potential of innovations regarded as having high potential within a specific sector. With the exception of the chemical industry, it becomes clear that the visions presented by industry actors display greater confidence towards decarbonisation than those generated by the academic community. Although various reasons may underpin the difference in perspective, such as scope or political assumptions used in the analysis, it offers the starting point for this Element to explore the visions of decarbonisation that are being advanced across these sectors and the kinds of imaginary worlds they are creating. In some cases, the nature of progress towards decarbonisation means that visions of decarbonised futures are far ahead of the realities (e.g. steel, plastic), and in these cases, our analysis seeks to examine the challenges which will be encountered in realising these

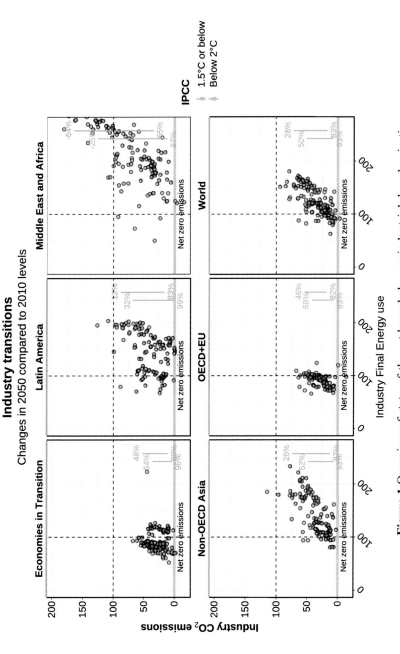

Figure 1 Overview of state-of-the-art knowledge on industrial decarbonisation

Source: Huppmann et al. (2018)

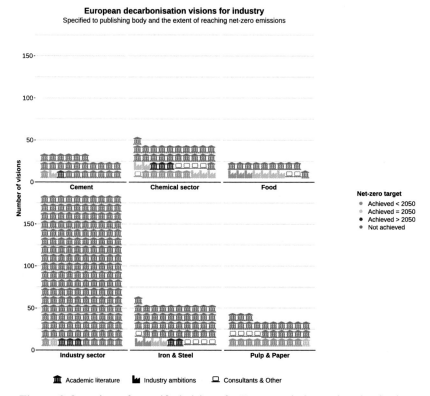

Figure 2 Overview of quantified visions for European industry decarbonisation, looking both at visions developed in academics (Greek temple) or industry (factory)
Sources: Allwood et al. 2010; Audsley et al. 2009; Bellevrat and Menanteau 2009; Broeren et al. 2014; CEFIC and Ecofys 2013; DECHEMA 2017; ECIU 2020; European Commission 2018a; Heaps et al. 2009; Milford et al. 2013; IEA 2009, 2016, 2017, 2018; Pardo et al. 2012; Van Ruijven et al. 2016; Van Sluisveld et al. 2018, 2020; WSP Parsons Brinckerhoff and DNV GL 2015a, 2015b, 2015c

visions in practice. In other sectors (e.g. meat, milk), decarbonisation realities are taking more concrete form, and our analysis seeks to examine how far different visions are coming to be borne out as the politics of decarbonisation takes hold.

While such scenarios and visions may at first hand appear to be purely scientific endeavours or the green clothes worn by industries with a vested interest in demonstrating their credentials in a net-zero world, they also serve other important cultural functions. The process of constructing an imaginary

Net zero climate target setting status

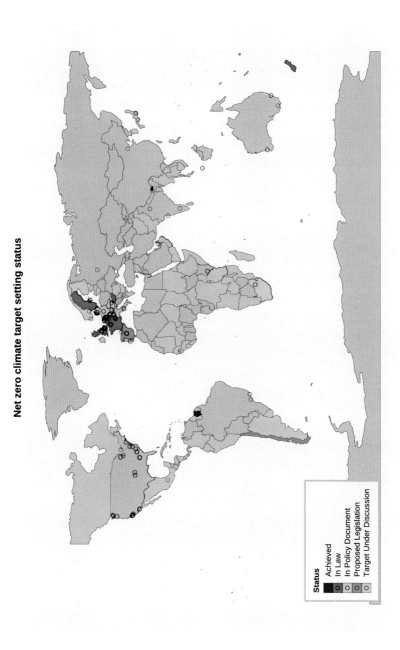

Status
- Achieved
- In Law
- In Policy Document
- Proposed Legislation
- Target Under Discussion

Figure 3 Overview of net-zero emission ambitions across the world (limited to countries and companies)

Source: ECIU 2020

world is often called 'worldbuilding', and across many contemporary phenomena, from energy forecasts, science-fiction novels, and video games, developing an imaginary setting with coherent qualities such as ecology, geography, and politics is a key task. Imaginary worlds have an open-ended and work-in-progress nature. They are also multi-authored, with stories written by different actors set in the same world. New agents of change, locations, and characters are continually being added. Despite the overarching narrative which forms the backbone of a climate-neutral Europe by 2050 (that we have managed to meet the Paris Agreement target of limiting global warming to 1.5 degrees), it seems clear that a climate-neutral Europe is not a single story but a mix of elements which can sustain multiple interrelated characters and their stories. Across this Element, we find radical visions for future trajectories, thriving innovations that might scale and get momentum, but also sobering realities of why we are stuck in a fossil world and why envisioning and realising alternative pathways are so difficult.

Real Transitions?

Turning these imaginary worlds into reality is no easy task. Since the 2015 Paris Agreement, a growing number of countries, cities, and companies have made pledges to reduce their carbon emissions to zero before or by 2050. The most progressive ambitions and commitments to date are to be found in Europe. Europe has a large concentration of those countries that have embedded a net-zero emission objective in policy or legislation, such as Sweden establishing a net-zero emission target for 2045 in the Swedish climate policy framework (Ministry of the Environment and Energy 2018), the United Kingdom for 2050 in the Climate Change Act 2008 (2050 Target Amendment) Order 2019 (2019), and France for 2050 in the Energy and Climate Bill No. 1908 (2019). At the same time, several major multinationals in carbon-intensive areas of the economy that have their headquarters in Europe have also committed to net-zero emissions by 2050, such as in the cement (e.g. HeidelbergCement 2019), steel (e.g. ArcelorMittal 2020; ThyssenKrupp 2019), chemicals (e.g. AkzoNobel 2017), and food (e.g. Arla 2019a; Danone 2019) sectors, echoing a trend for net-zero commitments across the corporate sector globally.

Common to many projections of the future through which such targets are imagined to be achieved is a tendency to rely on a few stand-alone interventions for realising their ambitions. Zero-carbon pathways attribute a significant potential to interventions that introduce a radical new approach or innovation, with many uncertainties left unaddressed about the broader implications of the diffusion or acceptance of new technologies or applications in society. Without this consideration, a 'reality gap' emerges between the dreams of how low-carbon transitions can or must be achieved and the actually existing transitions that are taking place on the ground. In part, this 'reality gap' has arisen because our approaches to understanding transitions have tended to prioritise the role of technical and social innovations in generating disruption and overcoming inertia without paying due attention to the range of actors involved in sustaining and contesting high-carbon economies; issues of power, economy, and culture; questions of the materiality of the economies within which we are seeking to change; or their geographies. Singular interventions are often imagined to emerge on a blank social and political canvas, where the primary drivers are thought about in raw economic terms of price and competition. Yet the realities of transitions are both much more complex and much messier.

In this Element, we examine how initiatives that seek to achieve decarbonisation in the steel, paper, plastic, meat, and milk sectors work in practice – which agents of change are involved and how do they generate the power to overcome inertia and 'undo' the carbon economy. We seek to explore how transitions are shaped by the socio-materiality of different sectors – for example, does the malleability of plastic open it up for new economies, or does the liquidity of milk raise different challenges for its decarbonisation? And how are transitions being shaped by the political economies and geographies of the value chains and socio-technical systems within which these economies are embedded? By drawing attention to the realities of transitions in a variety of carbon-intensive sectors of the economy, this Element aims to open up the question of what will be needed, by whom, and when, in order to realise the ambition of net-zero economies in Europe and beyond.

2 Steel

Few of us think about the presence and significance of steel in our everyday lives. As an alloy of iron and carbon, steel is the most widely used metal in the world, and we depend on it for a wide range of products and services. From the reinforced concrete and beams that support much of our modern built environment to the vehicles through which we are increasingly globally mobile and from machinery that produces consumer goods to the tin cans in which perishable products are stored, steel underpins much of what we take for granted. Given its ubiquity and longevity – from a decade or so in a car to potentially a hundred years or more in a building – the typical amount of steel locked up in advanced economies where demand is saturating is estimated to be between 10 and 15 tonnes per person. The global average is 4.2 tonnes per person, and this is expected to increase to nearly 6.5 tonnes per person in 2050 (IEA 2020a). Steel has not only been of material importance to the making of contemporary economies but also historically critical to their political economies. Historically, steelmaking has been both a matter of national security and a symbol of modernity, industrialisation, and progress through its use for industrial development, building infrastructures, and the urban landscapes that came to dominate the twentieth century.

Yet, despite the central role that steel plays in our lives, our use of steel is not often framed as an environmental concern. Extraction of iron ore, like other forms of mining, and pollution from primary production may cause significant damage to local environments, but it is the carbon emissions of steel production that are increasingly coming into focus. The two dominant routes for producing steel are: (i) the primary or blast furnace (BF) route using iron ore and coke, produced from high-quality coal, to produce virgin steel, and (ii) the secondary or electric arc furnace (EAF) route which uses mainly recycled steel and electricity for producing new steel. Each currently primarily depends on fossil fuel energy, with the primary route using about 8–10 times more energy than the secondary route (IEA 2020a). The steel industry accounts for 7 per cent of global carbon dioxide emissions, mainly through emissions from the primary route. As an economic sector with high levels of dependency on coal, the interests of the steel sector have long been aligned with those of the fossil fuel industry. The European Coal and Steel Community has led to the EU as we know it today. It was first proposed by the French Foreign Minister Robert Shuman in 1950 and subsequently established through the Treaty of Paris, which at the time of the 1951 included Belgium, France, Italy, Luxembourg, the Netherlands, and West Germany. Despite the cessation of this Treaty in 2002, the EU still has strong political and economic interests in the futures of both sectors, with a 40 MEUR Research Fund for Coal and Steel that specifically supports research and innovation projects in the areas of coal and steel.

As with other energy- and emission-intensive industries, steel has so far been sheltered from the effects of energy and climate policy through energy tax reductions and the free allocation of emissions allowances in the EU's

Emissions Trading Scheme. As long as the target in sight was an overall reduction of GHG emissions by 20–40 per cent by 2020 or 2030, the steel industry felt no urgent pressure to act. The Paris Agreement and the associated necessity for zero or even negative emissions have changed the playing field. As economies across Europe seek to embrace net-zero goals, there is growing pressure on the industry to show how it can play a role, and its long-term relation with the coal industry is increasingly under pressure. In the rest of this section, we examine how visions of technical progress dominate scenarios for decarbonising the steel sector, the ways in which both material and social realities are shaping ongoing efforts to realise these visions on the ground, and the extent to which there is any real prospect for a decarbonised steel economy in the future.

Visions

When it comes to imagining the future, the vision of the steel industry is an expansive one with crude steel production expected to continue a trajectory of expansion from 850 Mtonne in 2000 to 1,869 Mtonne in 2019 towards 2,600 Mtonne by the end of the twenty-first century (Pauliuk et al. 2013) driven by the expansion of infrastructure and buildings in the global South. Achieving such levels of expansion while also encountering carbon constraints has led those within the steel industry to focus primarily on technological pathways through which decarbonisation can be achieved. First and foremost, hopes have been invested in the possibilities of carbon capture and use (CCU) or storage (CCS), by which carbon emissions produced in the making of steel are either put to use in new products or securely stored and prevented from reaching the atmosphere. The second pathway has focused on the potential of electrification or indirect electrification through using hydrogen as a reduction agent in the conversion of iron ore to steel. At the same time, it is increasingly recognised that existing steel stocks hold promise as the infrastructures, built environments, and goods in which they are currently held come to the end of their life, potentially releasing significant levels of scrap steel that can be recycled. The share of scrap-based steel in total production is expected to increase from about one-quarter today to more than half by 2060 as the stock, and subsequently, the availability of scrap increases (Pauliuk et al. 2013). The third vision for decarbonised steel futures then rests on the reuse of steel such that no new virgin steel is required in the economy. Much less prominent and usually emerging outside of the steel industry itself, the fourth vision for steel futures is one that rests on making it less important to the economy through processes of substitution. In particular, whether and how to replace steel in the built environment – currently one of its main expanding markets – is attracting increasing attention.

Capture the Carbon

The basic vision of CCS, or 'smart carbon usage' as the industry refers to it (EUROFER 2019), is to capture carbon dioxide and store it underground to prevent it from being released into the atmosphere. The idea of CCS was first suggested in 1977 (Marchetti 1977), and it has mainly been considered in relation to the continued use of fossil fuels in power production. Expectations for global CCS deployment in the power sector were high in the early 2000s as it offered an economic future for the fossil fuel industry and power plants despite the necessity to reduce carbon dioxide emissions. However, the rapid development of renewable energy technologies, notably solar and wind, as well as the cost of CCS and a sceptical public has resulted in waning political support and interest for CCS in power production, such that at the time of writing, there has been no large-scale deployment of this technology.

Despite its infancy, the CCS idea was picked up by the steel industry as exemplified by the European Ultra- Low carbon dioxide steelmaking (ULCOS) research programs 2004–2015, involving all major European steel companies and co-funded by EU (Quader et al. 2016). ULCOS explored and tested several technologies, but the focus of its effort was on developing different concepts that included CCS, with names such as ULCOS-BF, HIsarna, and ULCORED. The main aim was to reduce emissions by at least 50 per cent, that is, from about 2 tons of carbon dioxide per ton of steel to about 1 ton of carbon dioxide. The largest emission reductions among those options, about 80 per cent, were shown to be possible by combining the HIsarna technology with CCS, a solution championed by Tata Steel.

With CCU, the idea is to capture carbon dioxide or carbon monoxide, mainly from BF gas, and use the carbon as a building block for chemicals and hydrocarbon fuels such as ethanol and methanol. Prominent examples include the Steelanol project by ArcelorMittal and the Carbon2Chem project involving ThyssenKrupp. CCU offers an attractive vision in which the words and images of 'carbon-neutral steelmaking', 'smart carbon usage', and 'circular economy' through 'carbon valorisation' are used in industry communications rather than CCU (see e.g. ArcelorMittal 2020; Tönjes et al. 2019). The ArcelorMittal vision of 'Smart Carbon' even goes as far as to label the ethanol produced as 'bioethanol': '[W]e are building an industrial-scale demonstration plant to capture carbon off-gases from the blast furnace and convert it into 80 million litres of bio-ethanol a year' (2020: 5). This claim is made under the dubious pretence that future BF gas can contain only 'circular carbon from the end of life plastics and from sustainable biomass' (ArcelorMittal 2020: 4). The Carbon2Chem project envisions a broader range of chemicals (methanol, ammonia, etc.) from BF gases and involves several large chemical companies. It has been granted an impressive 60 MEUR of funding from the German government for the first laboratory phase 2016–2020. The vision includes carbon dioxide-neutral steel, circular economy, and getting higher-value products from BF gases (Tönjes et al. 2019).

Electrification

Assuming ongoing growth in primary steel production, the alternative to CCS and CCU is to use hydrogen as a reduction agent or electricity directly in electrolytic processes. These two types of technologies hold the promise that primary steelmaking can become completely fossil-free. In this vision, the electricity and hydrogen are assumed to be produced from renewable resources. The steel industry would become a key part of the 'hydrogen economy' – a long-touted vision for a clean energy future. Hydrogen direct reduction builds on extensive previous experience of direct reduction using natural gas. The idea of using hydrogen to strip the oxygen from iron oxides to produce iron and water (as a by-product) is rather old, although it was not until 2016 that this hydrogen vision gained serious traction with the Swedish companies Vattenfall (electricity), LKAB (iron ore mining), and SSAB (steelmaker) announcing their plans for their Hydrogen Breakthrough Ironmaking Technology (HYBRIT) for fossil-free steelmaking. Several other steelmakers have followed suit since to announce the development of various hydrogen projects.

One potential implication of the hydrogen or renewable electricity vision of decarbonised steel is that it may serve to rework the geographies of production. Current steel plants are in places to which iron ore and coking coal can be easily transported. In the future, it may be advantageous to produce iron in regions endowed with renewable energy. One such region is Australia where, in several places, there are good coexisting solar and wind resources. In addition, Australia has large iron ore resources, producing 38 per cent of the world's iron ore and is a large exporter (Wood et al. 2020). In this vision, Australia's current 'carbon workers' in coal mining or oil and gas extraction are to find future jobs in green iron and steelmaking. In such a vision, briquetted iron can be exported, possibly mixed with scrap, and made into steel in EAFs in other parts of the world where steel mills already exist, or the steel can be produced in Australia and then exported.

Scrap Economies

Scrap has been a valuable asset and recycled ever since the Iron Age. Globally, around 80–90 per cent of the steel that goes out of use is already recycled (IEA 2020a). Steel industry visions, as, for example, expressed in industry roadmaps, generally include the option of recycling even if it is not as central as the visions of CCS/CCU or hydrogen. Actors within the sector emphasise steel's material qualities and the possibility this affords to recycle it without losing quality. For example, the World Steel Association states that 'today's steel products will become tomorrow's cans, trains, bridges and buildings' (World Steel Association 2020), while the Swedish steel producers' association declares that '[s]teel is 100 % recyclable, for eternity' (Jernkontoret 2018: 16). The implication is that should demand for steel stabilise, there would, in principle, no longer be a need to mine for iron ore to produce primary steel. In this vision, which often accompanies the technological pathways for new steel mentioned previously, it is relatively straightforward for steel to move through a cycle of production, static use, and release for recycling. Given that primary steelmaking uses much more energy than the secondary scrap-based route and that steel recycling can be powered by renewable electricity, the idea that scrap steel can be continually reused is central to visions of how the sector can bring its carbon footprint under control.

It is worth noting, however, that this scrap vision has largely pushed out a different, but related, vision of a low-carbon steel future: that which centres around the reuse of steel. As Santos and Lane (2017) demonstrate in relation to the building sector, the dominance of a vision in which scrap steel is put to new purposes should be attributed not only to steel's material qualities but also to the existence of a stable 'scrap regime' consisting of building owners, demolition companies, and state-based regulation and certification schemes, which continue to favour recycling over reuse visions. Nonetheless, there are examples where a reuse vision of steel is emerging. In Portland, Oregon, for example, the municipal authority has developed a 'deconstruction' fund to support the deconstruction rather than demolition of older buildings, such that useful materials can be taken and reused in the building sector (Metcalfe 2016). Analysis undertaken by the C40 Cities Climate Leadership Group suggests that by 2050, '[...] construction companies could reuse at least a quarter of structural steel through improved coordination between the demolition and construction phases' (C40 2019: 32).

Move over Steel?

In addition to steel visions, the substitution of other materials, particularly timber, in building construction is attracting increasing attention. This has been facilitated by two processes. First, there has been a growing concern for the emissions associated with the built environment. Second, the growth of material innovations that have the potential to enable timber to replace steel, such as the development of cross-laminated timber (CLT) – a technology that was developed in Austria during the 1990s motivated by the need for sawmills to develop higher-value products (Brandner et al. 2016). CLT consists of several layers of solid wood laminations glued together crosswise and can be produced in various lengths and shapes in elements that are stable and load bearing. This has made wooden construction function on a par with steel, such that even wooden skyscrapers are now possible as exemplified by the 18-storey and 85-meter-high Mjøstårnet in Norway completed in 2019 and now the tallest wood-framed building in the world. Elsewhere, there continues to be an arms race between who will build the next tallest 'plyscraper', with a plethora of projects either proposed or under construction across major cities around the world, including a 180-meter hybrid timber/steel tower proposed in Sydney and a 350-meter-high one in Tokyo.

Figure 4 The 85-meter-high Mjøstårnet in Norway. The building's structure is composed of both glued laminated timber and cross-laminated timber
Source: The photo is provided by Moelven 2019

This vision of the plyscraper has come together through a loose coalition of rural (e.g. vertically integrated forestry companies such as Stora Enso and Sumitomo and regional politicians) and urban actors (city officials and leading architectural firms), who see in CLT the potential to revive both rural economies and tackle carbon emissions from the urban built environment at the same time. Politicians in the US state of Oregon went as far as to declare CLT 'essential' to the state's economic interests, changing regulations that would allow higher timber towers (in primarily urban areas) to help the state's ailing rural forestry industry (Manning 2019). What is particularly notable is how this vision of the new 'age of timber' is propelled, through glossy architectural renderings – often reproduced in international news items on the latest plyscraper announcement – that emphasise timber's aesthetic qualities over its low-carbon credentials. Through timber's aesthetics, such representations thus seek to present a new desirable urban future, with steel, in the words of New York City Mayor Bill de Blasio (2019), little more than a remnant of the past:

> *We're going to make very clear that the kind of the glass and steel buildings of the past, and some bluntly were being built very recently, are just not going to be allowed anymore.*

Realities

When it comes to decarbonisation, steel presents some cold hard realities. It remains a sector deeply embedded in the political economy of nation-states, such that despite a large gap between existing capacity for steel production (2362 Mt) and actual production (1848 Mt), it is expected that the provision of global capacity will increase (OECD 2020), driven among other things by Chinese state strategy and concerns in India and the Middle East not to be dependent on foreign imports (Brun 2016). Demand for virgin steel is not then only driven by the nature of the market but also by geopolitics and the central place that the steel sector occupies in many states. This is a status that is not only politically but materially 'locked-in'. The BF, the heart of the primary production route, has been used and continuously developed, upscaled, and refined for hundreds of years. It is used in large, complex, energy-efficient, and highly integrated steel plants that may also include coke ovens, basic oxygen furnaces, EAFs, casting, and rolling mills. This, together with capital intensity, economies of scale, and long investment cycles, creates a strong carbon lock-in that has co-evolved with institutional regimes over decades and centuries (Seto et al. 2016; Unruh 2000). As such, to date, the visions for steel futures discussed earlier remain largely confined to competing claims over the future of steel, and our discussion focuses on how these visions are encountering various limits as they seek to gain traction in the real world.

Cold Comfort from Carbon Capture?

CCS could in theory allow for the continued use of BFs, but the realities are that it is not viable to capture more than perhaps 50–60 per cent of emissions through retrofitting existing plants (Quader et al. 2016). The multitude of source points of carbon dioxide emissions across mills, retrofit costs, and limited physical space constrain the potential and efficiency of CCS. It increases production costs without any clear additional benefits beyond emissions reduction. The HIsarna process, which requires new build plants, in combination with CCS, can reach zero emissions if about 20 per cent of the fossil coal feedstock is replaced with biogenic carbon or charcoal. This makes HIsarna an attractive option, but the question remains whether it will be perceived as green steel by markets, regulators, and policymakers as it still relies on fossil feedstock. This technology dates back to the 1960s but was revived in 1990 to improve energy efficiency and reduce emissions by replacing coke with powdered coal in a different type of vessel than the conventional BF. It was revived again through the ULCOS programmes since it is more suitable for CCS than the BF. Another option is hydrogen steelmaking using natural gas and CCS to produce ′blue′ hydrogen instead of ′grey′ hydrogen where the carbon is emitted. Both ′grey′ and ′blue′ hydrogen are currently less expensive than the ′green′ hydrogen envisioned in renewable electricity futures.

Despite the industry framing of CCU as promising means for carbon-neutral steelmaking and smart carbon usage, such a process is still dependent on the use of fossil carbon in the making of steel and on the production of carbon-intensive by-products whose market is as yet uncertain. It may lead to 30–50 per cent lower emissions – for example, the steel off-gasses can be used as feedstock in the chemical industry, which then avoids using other fossil feedstock – but it does not lead to zero emissions. While the steelmaker may be relieved of their responsibilities for this carbon, the question as to what the downstream chemicals company makes of this prospect is as yet unknown and untested. Indeed, such a shift may suggest that the decarbonisation of one carbon-intensive sector does little more than to move the carbon around the economy like so many deckchairs on the Titanic. Given the regulatory conditions and financial implications of producing large volumes of carbon within the EU ETS, how the accounting for carbon and the allocation to different products should be done in cases like this is already highly contested. As such, it is uncertain whether technological innovations that are likely to generate further strain in this system are likely to be successful.

Clean Steel and Renewable Electricity Futures

Hydrogen-based primary steelmaking appears to offer some promise, if only under the assumption that affordable, emissions-free, and preferably renewable, electricity is available in sufficient quantities. Production costs may increase, but the option offers interesting co-benefits to electricity systems through flexible electricity demand and hydrogen storage. Forecasts suggest that this could require an additional 210–355 TWh/yr of electricity in Europe if fully implemented (Material Economics 2019). This is equivalent to 20–35 per cent of current EU industrial electricity demand (about 1,000 TWh/yr), corresponding to an increase by 7–12 per cent of the total EU electricity generation (about 3,000 TWh/yr). The large amounts of energy needed for stripping iron oxides of their oxygen are unavoidable and underscore the importance of recycling and material efficiency to reduce the need for primary steelmaking.

The high electricity demand in the 'green' hydrogen vision also has wider implications. It will make economic sense to locate primary production in places that are rich in low-cost renewable electricity from wind and solar. At present, iron ore, coke, and coking coal are shipped to steel plants around the world. But renewable electricity and hydrogen are harder to move over such long distances. It is possible to ship hydrogen carriers such as ammonia (NH_3), methane (CH_4), and methanol (CH_3OH), but it makes more sense to locate the iron – or steelmaking near the renewable electricity and then ship the briquetted iron or the steel for further processing and finishing (Wood et al. 2020). However, what may seem to be the most efficient from an engineering perspective will, in reality, be balanced against national political-economic interests and concerns for resource security or well-being of regional communities and jobs.

The HYBRIT project starting in 2016 exemplifies the importance of these material and geographical realities. The steel company SSAB was faced with the prospect of refurbishing their coke oven and a BF. The electricity company Vattenfall was looking for new markets for their emissions-free Swedish electricity, and LKAB has the only iron ore mine in Europe. Vattenfall and LKAB are state-owned, and all companies are headquartered in Sweden, facilitating short decision paths and serving to build trust. In the light of Swedish climate policy and the Paris Agreement, ULCOS's ambition of reducing carbon emissions by about 50 per cent were not low-carbon enough for SSAB who wanted to reach zero emissions (Tönjes et al. 2019). Although it was still unclear how to build the value chain and business models, it was decided to go for hydrogen reduction and for a joint venture called HYBRIT Development AB. A one-ton-per-hour pilot plant went into operation in 2020. It was also decided in 2020 that the large-scale demonstration plant originally planned for 2035 should be bought forward to be in place by 2026 in order to accelerate the transition.

Recycling Constrained

Scenarios for future steel demand model widely different futures, from possible decline to increases in demand in the next 20 years. These overall changes in demand are expected to affect the quantity of scrap steel in circulation. A reduction in demand is associated with a more scrap-based (70 per cent versus 40 per cent today) steel economy, but even under this scenario it is predicted that in 2050 the EU will still need to produce or import millions of tons of primary steel (Material Economics 2019). However, the realities of the recycling vision are further complicated when we consider how the ideal of frictionless material flows run up against the materialities, temporalities, and geographies of steel. In terms of materialities, a key challenge to recycling is copper contamination which may render the scrap-based steel unsuitable for high-quality applications, for example, those which require high-strength and lightweight steel. Thus, the claim that steel is '100 per cent recyclable' (Jernkontoret 2018: 95; World Steel Association 2020) must be taken with a pinch of salt. Changes in product design and improved separation processes at end-of-life are important to increase the share of scrap-based steel. However, constraints on recycling are not simply technical in nature. Steel's material qualities – in this case its long lifespan – also shape the potential for recycling due to the ways it intersects with temporalities. As Santos and Lane (2017) note, important decisions about the use of steel in buildings are made at three stages of its life cycle: demolition, recycling, and construction. However, due to the long lifespans of buildings, decisions at different stages of their lives are generally made independently of the others. Decisions about design, construction, renovations, re-purposing, and demolition of buildings can be spread over more than 100 years, making coordination difficult and creating barriers to the ease with which steel could be recycled. In addition to this temporal challenge, there is also an important geographic dimension that shapes the prospects for recycled steel, for as with other resources for steel, 'resource recovery engenders highly complex and brokered forms of governance' (Crang et al. 2013: 12). The spatial organisation of the value chain – local scrap-recycling regimes embedded in a fragmented global regime – shapes what steel gets collected, where it gets processed, and when it gets used. And although some aspects of the recycled steel flows can be governed through national regulation or standards, such efforts run up against a global landscape that shapes the pathways and possibilities for a more sustainable steel future (Santos and Lane 2017).

The Coming Age of Wood?

Despite the recent interest in substituting steel with timber of other materials, particularly in buildings, the so-called coming age of wood is not without its challenge(r)s and complexities. To understand the challenges that timber faces in replacing steel, it is worth considering the particular material's qualities and how these are communicated in order to position timber as a desirable replacement. A focus on materials and materiality draws attention to issues such as how much weight a wooden beam can hold or how long it takes to deteriorate. While the emerging plyscrapers in European and North American cities help demonstrate what timber is capable of, as wood technology is still developing, errors will also be made along the way. Such as in Oregon, where a section of the third floor of a timber building under construction gave way and crashed onto the floor below (Manning 2019). Material substitution is far from straightforward, requiring new ways of assessing material qualities, the reskilling of actors, and renewed supply chain coordination.

As new technologies or materials emerge, the promise of 'the next big thing' thus soon comes up against the systems and practices that are already in place. How does the weight that CLT can hold compare to steel? What is its lifespan? Is there a risk of fire? And, for our purposes, is it actually more 'green' than steel? The deemed suitability of materials is strongly shaped through standards and regulations, established forms of calculation through which it becomes possible to compare timber with other materials (Santos and Lane 2017). While there are multiple ongoing attempts to pin down timber's carbon benefits, for example, through the development of new standards for life cycle analysis (LCA) and other calculative practices, calculating the carbon impact of timber remains challenging. Although new standards provide an overarching framework to calculate emissions from construction, it has been left to users to decide on the system boundaries for their analysis (Giesekam and Pomponi 2017). These details and choices are often not made publicly available, making it difficult to externally evaluate and compare the carbon impact of different materials. However, CLT's growing prominence means it is increasingly coming under scrutiny in these debates.

Prospects

Steel will likely remain the most widely used metal in society for decades to come. If energy supplies are decarbonised to meet climate targets, an increasing share of global carbon dioxide emissions will emanate from basic materials production. Here, the steel sector is one of the major emitters, and with production predicted to increase over time it is likely to be subject to increasing pressure to contribute to a climate-neutral Europe. For many in the steel sector itself, focused primarily on technical and economic dynamics, prospects for decarbonising steel through a combination of demand and supply measures appear promising. Yet such a view tends to obscure historical legacies and inertia, developments in other sectors, and political-economic conditions that will condition the shapes that steel decarbonisation can take.

Signs of increasing interest in material use and embodied emissions are now becoming visible. Various initiatives for green procurement, including The Climate Group's SteelZero campaign, climate requirements in building construction, and LCA-based building declarations such as BREEAM and LEED (European Commission 2020; IISD 2018; The Climate Group 2021) signify that some in the building sector are coming to realise that political attention is increasingly directed beyond direct energy emissions and to the material footprint of their 'low-carbon' buildings. Similarly, interest in green steel for cars and other vehicles may also increase as the share of emissions from fuels and electricity decline and the share of material embodied emissions of total vehicle life-cycle emissions increases. There is, however, yet no common agreement on what is meant by ´green steel´. Will it mean emissions-free steel based on CCS and ´blue´ hydrogen or is it only steel produced using renewable energy and ´green´ hydrogen?

Yet, making changes to steel's carbon economy remains a challenging endeavour. Technological pathways offer some possibilities but are far from the smooth transitions that industry-based visions imply. With neither CCS nor CCU appearing to offer currently proven economically or politically viable interventions, attention appears to be increasingly turning to the promise that hydrogen-based processes hold. On the other hand, in locations with limited access to cheap electricity, CCS may still be seen as an option for steelmaking, especially when considering also effects on regional communities and jobs. Natural gas direct reduction is an attractive option in gas-rich regions, and it is well suited to be equipped with CCS. For hydrogen-based processes, it is the abundance of cheap, renewable electricity upon which so much turns. Where nation-states have been making advances in the provision of renewable electricity, perhaps new kinds of steel–electricity alliances can be formed through which the decarbonisation of one sector can lead to significant low-carbon transition pathways across another. Equally, forecasts for a growth in the use of recycled materials or materials efficiency are also dependent on many actors outside of the steel sector – scrap metal merchants, intermediary organisations, designers, engineers, car manufacturers, and many more. So too with substitution – designing steel out of our economy will require multiple innovations not only in terms of design and architecture but also in how we think about and imagine the modern world from the provision of infrastructure to the urban skyline.

Even if more efficient and circular material flows materialise, the world as well as the EU is forecast to have a continued dependence on primary steel production, currently the main sources of emissions. The realities of a decarbonised steel economy, therefore, point towards the necessity of supply-side technological solutions on the pathway ahead. Furthermore, given that the use of CCS, hydrogen, and electrification will most likely make steel more expensive, these are unlikely to be forthcoming in a sector long dependent on state support, such that strong government incentives and green market demand are needed for the steel industry to begin to deploy these options at scale.

3 Plastic

A modern society without plastic is almost unthinkable. Found in packaging, clothing, cables, cars, and a zillion other everyday items, plastic has become a ubiquitous element of life. Versatile, durable, lightweight, strong, and inexpensive. Our contemporary love of plastic is understandable. It reduces costs and brings technological advances that can save energy and avoid food waste. At the same time, the production, consumption, and disposal of plastic are fraught with problems. Plastic is fossil based, often designed for single-use and does not degrade or recycle easily, sparking an increasing concern about a 'plastic crisis' by social movements, media, and policymakers (Nielsen et al. 2020). The 'plastic crisis' is increasingly understood as a multifaceted phenomenon connecting fossil dependency, toxicity, disposability, pollution, and permanence (Chertkovskaya et al. 2020). In many current debates, the question of plastic waste and pollution has come to be the most visible. As much as 60 per cent of plastic waste is estimated to have been discarded into the natural environment, amassing in oceans and on land, polluting habitats, and harming different species (Geyer et al. 2017). In the context of climate change, it is the fossil content of plastics that are in the foreground both in terms of their high demand for fossil-fuel energy in production and the ways in which, once broken down by degradation or incineration, the carbon molecules that plastics are made of are released back to accumulate in the atmosphere.

Plastics belong to a wider group of petrochemicals, telling of how plastics are made and have come to be embedded within a larger petro-industrial complex. Plastic manufacturing largely relies on fossil fuels, with 99 per cent of the feedstock being fossil-based (Hamilton and Feit 2019) and plastic production relying on fossil-based energy. In 2009, 7–8 per cent of global oil and gas production went into plastic manufacture (4 per cent as feedstock and 3–4 per cent as energy). This is projected to increase to 20 per cent by 2050 (Ellen MacArthur Foundation 2016). Oil companies have invested heavily in the production of petrochemicals to seek new markets for their assets (CIEL 2017). With ethane and propane regarded as by-products of petroleum refining and natural-gas extraction (e.g. through fracking), the more oil and gas that is extracted the cheaper it will be to produce plastics. The embedding of plastics within the global economy of fossil fuel production has made it difficult for alternative ways to produce plastics to emerge.

Currently, the primary use of plastics (40 per cent) is to wrap and protect food and other goods (Ellen MacArthur Foundation 2016). Since the mid-twentieth century, plastics have been embedded in modern consumption cultures of convenience, such as the on-the-go culture, disposability, and the modern supermarket. Historically, the emergence and growth of plastics is interwoven with the growth of packaged economies and the development of 'self-service'. From the 1950s and onwards, the idea of 'self-service' within modern retail generated expectations around how goods should be packaged and arranged within easy reach of the consumer. Packaging became a powerful device through which consumers could serve themselves, which led to large-scale transformations of retail, markets, and spaces of consumption (Hagberg 2016). To Hawkins (2018), the spread of plastic packaging occurred at the intersection of numerous industries and everyday practices – food production, transportation, retailing, marketing, and consumption – rendering them both necessary and normal.

This might be about to change. It started with the tiny object of the plastic carrier bag. Unlike other plastic objects, carrier bags have been subjected to more than a decade of governmental (and non-governmental) initiatives to limit their usage, totalling around 160 public policies at the national and municipality level (Nielsen et al. 2019). Plastics are becoming in a sense unwelcome. Yet, there is no coherent vision of what it might mean to realise a decarbonised plastics economy. Business organisations, governments, international organisations, scientific advisory boards, and social movements all differ on what a decarbonised plastics economy looks like and what needs to be done to get there. Further, the challenges of bringing these visions into reality are signifi-cant – especially under conditions of an enduring fossil fuel economy. In the rest of this section, we explore these fragmented visions, sobering realities, and the prospects for removing carbon from this essential part of our everyday lives.

Visions

Partly due to its multiplicity and ubiquity (generating thousands of possible agents and sites of intervention), and partly due to the difficulty of imagining a viable alternative that can fulfil the role that plastic plays in everyday life, what it means to create a decarbonised plastic economy is anything but settled. Some envision a 'bio-based plastics economy' where plastics are not produced through fossil fuels, but, for example, through agricultural products (e.g. starches and sugars from crops), cellulose, bio-waste, or even carbon dioxide. Others envision that more could be done with less (virgin) plastic. In such a 'circular plastics economy', plastics never become waste but are instead recycled and put to use in producing plastics again. Finally, there are emerging visions of a 'life without plastics'. Here, we take a closer look at these visions – to better understand who is making these visions, how they are made, and the role they play in shaping transitions.

Bio-Based Futures

Given an opportunity to produce plastics differently, a vision of a bio-based plastics economy has taken hold. In bio-based plastic economies, plastics are used in the same way as today. It is not a pathway that challenges our use of plastics, nor does it require more plastics to be recycled. To move towards such an economy is an intriguing opportunity for European policymakers, for it starts to disconnect plastics from its dependency on fossil fuels in turn reducing dependency on foreign oil and opening up new possibilities for channelling subsidies to different constituencies, such as to support rural development through biorefineries. In the preparatory roadmap of the European Commission's strategy on plastics, a 'high dependence on virgin fossil feed-stock' was identified as one of the three main interrelated issues that the strategy aimed to address (European Commission 2017). The roadmap highlights the need to work on alternative feedstocks, technical barriers to feedstock recyc-ling, and incentives for feedstock diversification. However, in the final *Plastics Strategy* (European Commission 2018b), the emphasis on plastics' fossil con-tent shifted in favour of addressing plastic pollution, leading this particular vision to be devalued in favour of 'circular solutions' (see later in the text). The niche-character of bioplastics, the uncertainties of land-use questions, and a fear of repeating previous mistakes where biofuels with high negative climate impacts were promoted within the bioeconomy framework appear to have driven this change (DG ENV Official 2018).

These difficulties may explain why it is not very common to find arguments supporting a bioplastic economy on their own, but rather a part of a broader strategy to decarbonise the plastics system. For the German organisation Nova, bioplastics are a 'drop-in' solution that only requires moderate changes in production lines, without the need to replace too much infrastructure and refineries. Such growing economies around 'biogenic carbon' will create European jobs and competitiveness. Nova Institute suggests that out of the total raw material demand of the chemical industry in Europe, the 14 per cent share covered by biomass in 2015 could double or triple by 2050 (Carus and Raschka 2018). In their calculations towards a fossil-free plastics economy, out of a 1,200 global Mt production in 2050, the Nova Institute envisage how 750 Mt could be covered by recycling or recycled feedstock. The remaining virgin production of 135 Mt would come from biomass and 325 Mt carbon-dioxide-based production (CCU). While fossil-based plastics in this scenario become less viable as prices for fossil-fuels rise, bio-plastics visions still often rely on the carbon economy for their viability.

Closing the Loop

Many ideas of a circular plastics economy have come to the foreground in recent years. It is a variegated but encompassing vision, backed by many influential industries and with few opponents. A closed loop of plastics with 100 per cent recycling would reduce the need for virgin feedstock, increase overall resource efficiencies, and prevent carbon from reaching the atmosphere. Currently, circa 40 per cent of plastic waste in the EU is collected for recycling (PlasticsEurope 2019) but not all of that is actually recycled. Of all the 8.3 billion tons of plastics ever produced, only 9 per cent has been recycled (Geyer et al. 2017). To achieve 100 per cent recycling, we would need to see massive recycling schemes being implemented, both mechanical (reusing the plastic material) and chemical (reusing the chemicals). These schemes would have to be mandatory, not just for plastic packaging but for plastic across the economy, for example, in the automotive industry, textiles, and construction.

The European Commission's ambition is that by 2030 all packaging in the EU market is either reusable or recyclable in a cost-effective manner and that more than half of the plastic waste in EU is recycled (European Commission 2018b). Similarly, Stockholm-based influential consultancy firm Material Economics (2019) envisaged in their *Industrial Transformation 2050* report that by 2050, heavy industry sectors in EU would achieve net-zero carbon through the circulation of materials. For plastics, this means a combination of mechanical and chemical recycling to make end-of-life plastics a major feedstock for the European plastic industry. The chemical industry itself has put out similar ideas, as found, for example, in *Molecule Managers: A journey into the Future of Europe with the European Chemical Industry* (CEFIC 2019). In this report, the control of chemicals is key to strengthening the EU economically and diplomatically. Recycling is also increased dramatically (three-fold) in the IEA's 2018 scenario *The Future of Petrochemicals: Towards more sustainable plastics and fertilisers* (Fernandez-Pales and Levi 2018), as well as in the global NGO the Ellen MacArthur Foundation's (n.d.) *Vision of a Circular Economy for Plastic*. Despite its lack of coherence and often-heroic assumptions, it is this vision for a decarbonised plastics future that dominates the sector.

Less Is More

A rather different vision is that we use less plastic, mostly living our lives without it. Within social media, this has in the past years become popular through notions of plastics dieting, plastic-free months, and zero-waste stores. Living a life without plastics is central to the zero-waste movement that has recently gained momentum. One example is Bea Johnson, who started blogging about zero waste in 2010. She documented and kept a detailed tally of the annual amount of waste her household was generating (Johnson 2016). When word got out that a family of four could fit a year's worth of waste in a single mason jar, media interest picked up. Her 2013 book has been translated into more than 25 languages, and she now counts more than 350,000 social media followers and has featured more than 100 times on television. Already in 2010, *The New York Times* called Bea Johnson the 'priestess of waste-free living'. Another emerging trend is the plastic-free supermarket. What these stores have in common is an approach to retail that seeks to eliminate disposable packaging – especially plastics – and food waste. This requires customers to bring their own bags, containers, and jars and buy goods by weight according to how much they need. Despite being a seemingly marginal phenomenon in the retail sector, the significance of zero-waste retail is, however, not really about market share, but how it carries a vision of different food, plastics, and retail systems, as well as how they craft new relationships of producers and consumers.

Between 'circular plastics' and 'life without plastics', there are many suggestions for how less use of plastics could be achieved. The report by NGO Zero Waste Europe (2017), *Seizing the opportunity: Using plastic only where it makes sense*, called for tougher targets and eventually bans on many single-use plastic items. The message is that although increased recycling is welcome, Europe cannot recycle its way out of plastic pollution, instead, it must have a clear strategy to reduce plastic use. This requires designing things differently, substituting plastics with other materials (paper cotton bud sticks, steel bottles), and different forms of governance and regulation. It also involves changing habits and relations around reuse. The return of reuse is an integral part of the visions for a plastic-free world and has come to the forefront as one particular site of socio-technical innovation. The Ellen MacArthur Foundation (2019) envisions four general models that could change the mode of personal (plastic) packaging logistics: (1) return from home – packaging is picked up from home by a pickup service (e.g. by a logistics company); (2) refill at home – users refill their reusable container at home (e.g. with refills delivered through a subscription service); (3) refill on the go – users refill their reusable container away from home (e.g. at an in-store dispensing system); and (4) return on the go – users return the packaging at a store or drop-off point (e.g. in a deposit return machine or mailbox). One emerging innovation is around setting up a public library system for reusable items such as toys, clothes, and tools in order to drastically decrease demand for various items.

If 'bio-based plastics' was about producing plastics differently, 'life without plastics' is a reimagination of the whole system in which plastics is seen as essential and normal. These visions of less use are often focussed around getting rid of particular objects – bags, bottles, food packages, and single-use plastics – which are increasingly contested focal points for social movements and NGOs targeting plastic consumption (Nielsen et al. 2019). There are repeated calls for political authorities to regulate, for example, through taxes, levies, or otherwise getting rid of certain types of plastics applications (or additives and fillers) through bans or public procurement guidelines. The United Kingdom (UK), European Commission, and India have, in parallel, proposed legislation to reduce the consumption of a range of single-use plastic objects including plastic utensils, plates, and straws (Environmental Audit Committee 2018; European Commission 2018b).

Realities

Amidst these diverse and parallel visions of decarbonised plastic futures, the realities remain somewhat different as the petrochemical industry continues to invest heavily in the current system. In January 2019, Ineos, one of the biggest petrochemical companies in the world, announced that they had chosen Antwerp as their location for a new large-scale steam cracker, the key process for making plastics. It will be the first petrochemical investment of this scale in the EU for two decades. At first glance, Europe does not appear to be a favourable location for a fossil-fuel-driven petrochemical facility of this kind. Fossil fuel reserves in western Europe are almost depleted, the region is a mature market for plastics, and EU might be one of the most progressive players in the global efforts to mitigate both climate change and plastic pollution. Yet, the reasons for the persistence of petro-plastics become clearer when we realise that the proximity of fossil-fuel feedstocks is no longer an issue. European governments support investments into the LNG infrastructure, and the American shale gas boom makes cheap gas imports increasingly available (Hunter 2018). Further, despite falling under the EU Emission Trading System (EU ETS), many plastic production processes are officially regarded as a 'carbon leakage industry', which results in allowances largely being provided free of charge (European Commission 2015: 24). In addition, Flemish authorities subsidise the local petrochemical actors for the indirect costs of EU ETS (higher energy costs) (Flanders Agency of Innovation and Entrepreneurship 2019).

The production of plastics remains therefore highly ingrained in the EU economy and entwined with the petrochemical industry, such that even in Europe, where we might expect low-carbon transitions to be underway, we see a high-carbon economy continuing to be entrenched. Yet, nonetheless, we are witnessing emerging sites and forms of experimentation that are seeking to gain traction for decarbonised visions of plastic futures.

Fossil-Free Clothing?

Fossil-based synthetic fibres, such as polyester, elastane, and polyamide constitute an increasingly large part of the fibres produced to make our clothes yet often remain outside the critical gaze of fossil-fuel protestors. The pro-duction of oil-based fibres is estimated to consume 342 million barrels of oil annually, and the fashion industry is estimated to be responsible for 1.2 billion tonnes of carbon dioxide equivalent, more than that of international flights and maritime shipping combined (Ellen MacArthur Foundation 2017). Tierra is a Swedish outdoor clothing manufacturer who has made a jacket consisting of 100 per cent bio-based synthetic fibre called *Deterra*. The process of produ-cing the jacket started just after the international climate change agreement in Paris. The use of bio-based plastics in clothing is not new, but they are most commonly blended together with fossil plastic. There have been efforts made to recycle clothing plastics; however, there are so far few companies produ-cing clothing made by 100 per cent fossil-free fabrics. The innovation of *Deterra* is thus the exclusion of fossil fuels altogether in the choice of textiles, leading to the production of the very first 100 per cent fossil-free modern jacket.

Rather than designed to be a market success, the jacket was made to answer the question: is it possible to produce a 100 per cent fossil-free jacket? The jacket was born within a protected space and brought to the market by a dedicated company. Supply chains for textiles are complex and lack transparency, with a long list of suppliers and subcontractors spanning the globe. Making the jacket led Tierra to investigate along the value chain and find out the origin, production conditions, and social impacts of the bio-based material, though it proved impossible to identify where the castor beans used in its manufacture had been grown. This may be one reason why, compared to other emission-intensive industries, clothing has been relatively ungoverned. The Sustainable Apparel Coalition develops a set of standardised supply-chain measurement tools for the footwear, apparel, and textile industry. However, the organisation's sustainability measure, the Higgs Index, is not evaluated by an external organisation. The global non-profit organisation Textile Exchange focuses on collecting and disseminating best practices regarding farming, materials, processing, traceability, and product end-of-life. They provide standards to ensure sustainability claims (e.g. recycled materials, organic cotton). While standards like these are important for knowledge sharing across the value chain, they are not enough to provide a reliable framework for bio-based textile materials. Finding materials that substitute the range of qualities provided by plastic fibre, compounded with a lack of trust in the 'green' credentials of alternatives, means that decarbonising clothing through bio-based plastics seems unlikely to catch on.

Since work started on the jacket, bio-based synthetic fibres have become more commonplace both within the outdoor sector and in conventional clothing. Now you can find these materials in shoes, activewear, and eveningwear. Thus, although more 100 per cent bio-based forms of clothing have not been seen on the market, there have been some mainstreaming of fossil-free component parts. However, it remains a miniscule niche of the clothing market where recycled polyester has become the primary 'renewable' fabric of choice. There is also much hope for large-scale closed-loop recycling of materials, which would not force clothing producers to radically decrease volume or alter their business models. But many barriers remain, such as the mixing of fabrics, labour-intensive sorting, undisclosed chemical content, and the low price of virgin fibres. At the consumer end, the donation of clothes back to producers and to second-hand stores has increased in recent years – but the industry has not been able to integrate this waste-stream into their operation. Only one per cent of clothes collected through H&M's recycling initiative made it into new clothes. Overall, though, this secondary market has decimated clothes industries in the Global South.

Organising Alternatives

In contrast to the more techno-economic innovations further up the plastic value chain (such as new types of plastics or new ways of producing them) or further down (innovations in recycling and waste management), zero-waste supermarkets stand out for representing innovations of a more social nature. There is no complicated technology or infrastructure that enables them. Neither is the organisational and business model of the zero-waste store overly innovative in comparison to conventional supermarkets. Although many new stores of this type have been opening in recent years, they still represent a minuscule fraction of turnover in the retail sector. And yet, from the very first day of business, zero-waste grocery stores have received industry and press attention, scrutiny, and criticism on a level that is entirely disproportionate to their tiny footprint. In light of this, how should we understand the organisation of zero-waste retail and its transformative potential?

Some of the earliest zero-waste stores opened in the mid-2000s, with the first store in 2006 considered to be *Unpackaged* in London. Today, several hundreds of zero-waste stores exist across Europe, with Germany having more than a hundred. All zero-waste stores see themselves as symbolically connected to the global zero-waste movement. It is their intention to become a space for sharing knowledge, provide tools and data on zero-waste and bring together different constituencies. There is a shared understanding that waste itself is problematic and an indication of how modern society is living without respect for nature. Any amount of waste that is generated is an indication of unsustainability – the logical conclusion is therefore to eliminate it by tackling its root causes rather than to recycle this material through the economy.

Zero-waste supermarkets are very closely linked to the local environments in which they exist, and, as a result, few of the owners show aspirations towards scaling up the scope or reach of their organisation, potentially removing its links to specific contexts. In this regard, zero-waste supermarkets challenge the arrangements that characterise the world of modern, industrial, global retail, especially: global supply chains, cheap products, convenience, disposability, and powerful intermediaries. Their zero-waste message is that retail as a whole needs to reconsider global supply chains if they are serious about sustainability, and shift towards local, organic, seasonal, and predominantly vegetarian products. It is thus interesting how something so mundane as a grocery store can engage in such prefigurative politics. As a form of activism, prefiguration is concerned with the 'attempted construction of alternative or utopian social relations in the present' (Yates 2015: 1), thereby anticipating or partially actualising the ultimate goals of a movement. In the end, it is not merely to get rid of packaging but to reconfigure the relations and institutions of modern retail altogether and manifest them in the present.

Prospects

Plastics is omnipresent, yet despite all the recent attention it has received, it remains in many ways invisible. It has become an intrinsic part of our lives to the degree it is difficult for us to imagine a world without plastics or even notice its presence. At the same time, the presence of plastics is increasingly scrutinised. Across social realms, different industries and societal groups respond to the plastic crisis through particular initiatives that attempt to transform production processes and consumption practices towards a more sustainable plastics system in terms of carbon, waste, and pollution. The ability of such initiatives to induce and shape plastic transitions is not confined to the borders of the state but operates across different systems and arenas, for example, in design principles, industry standards, or social milieus sharing new sustainable plastic practices. Yet, we cannot escape the fact that plastic futures are intimately linked to the central position of oil and gas in the world and ultimately to economic growth. The use of plastics has for the last three decades grown faster than other bulk materials such as steel, glass, and paper with the only small drop in production rates occurring during recessions, such as during the 1973 oil crisis, the financial crisis of 2008, and in the wake of the Coronavirus pandemic of the early 2020s. Current climate change efforts, and the increased electrification of the global vehicle fleet, will lead to less demand for the combustion of oil and gas. The oil and gas industry thus envisage plastics to become an important source of revenue, as the oil giant Saudi Aramco's (solely owned by the Saudi Arabian state) recent acquisitions in the plastics industry suggest. In the last two decades, many national oil companies and other state-owned enterprises have increasingly invested in petrochemical production. The biggest plastic producers are in fact owned by China and Middle Eastern countries. As states become invested in the plastic industry, it is unlikely that decarbonisation in terms of bio-based plastics or reduced overall volume of production will be in the interest of these powerful actors.

In parallel to plastic futures being connected to the oil and gas industry, plastic is increasingly contested and politicised as a matter of choice for individuals to a global crisis demanding a global response. Voices are being raised for a plastic convention or agreement under the supervision of United Nations to address the cross-border challenges of governing plastic transitions (Borrelle et al. 2017). So far, this debate focuses on plastic waste and pollution. While these issues are in the limelight of public attention, they are inseparable from how plastics come into the world. To be a driving force for decarbonisation, a plastics convention would need to also address production and feedstock issues. Furthermore, much hope is invested in circular business models, where waste is fundamentally revaluated and used as an important resource in society. Many ideas, initiatives, and frameworks for such development have been put forward, and these are likely to shape developments to come. Visions of the circular economy tend to place agency for sustainability transitions wholly within industrial structures and processes, removing it from consumers, who are seen as driven only by considerations of convenience and cost. In contrast, zero-waste, a collective assemblage comprised of online influencers, local communities, and zero-waste grocery stores, point to individuals as important agents of change as both citizens and consumers. While zero-waste is about protest, circular economy is completely coherent with the existing growth and profitability narratives that are built on the hypothesis of 'decoupling' – effectively allowing for economic growth without environmental degradation.

In Jorge Gamboa's 'The tip of the iceberg' – an iconic image, circulated widely online before ending up on the cover of National Geographic – an upturned plastic bag floating in the water looks like an iceberg. The image is meant to illustrate that the waste we can see is just a fraction of the total amount of plastic in our oceans. It is symptomatic of the current situation where so much attention from policymakers, movements, citizens scholars, and even artists, is on plastic pollution. While Gamboa's image renders plastic pollution visible, it also obscures plastics' connection to fossil fuels. The same could indeed be said about EU's current plastic strategy. Could the EU, a region with diminishing fossil-fuel reserves, rise to the challenge and build momentum for transitions to a sustainable post-fossil plastics system? Oil giants currently bet that a major growth in plastics will enable them to make money despite the world moving towards low-carbon energy systems. On the face of it, rather than embracing the possibility of a post-fossil fuel plastic system the EU seems on course to favour a more incremental approach to plastic reduction, reuse, recycling, and bio-based production. The danger is that rather than serving as a means through which to carve out a pathway to decarbonisation, such an incremental approach will serve to further embed plastics in our lives and in turn sustain the fossil-fuel economy in the long run, reducing the possibilities for deep decarbonisation.

4 Paper

Paper is (still) king. Although we may store most of our photos on digital media and use credit cards for our grocery shopping, much of the information we rely on is still printed on paper for secure long-term storage while cash is still used on an everyday basis around the world. At the same time, how we use paper is changing. Fewer newspapers are being printed as readers move to online editions, while increases in online shopping mean that demand for paper packaging has soared. And books – such as this one – still hold a specific value to many people when held between two covers. Paper's qualities mean that different kinds have been used for a very long time – the history of papermaking in China dates back to the third century – and have remained similar in using plant fibres to produce sheets of paper for writing and drawing. The modern pulp and paper industry emerged in Europe during the industrial revolution and shifted the material foundation of the industry from plant fibres such as linen, hemp, and cotton to wood fibres which required new production processes (Alén 2018). Today, we use more than 400 million tons of paper every year globally – about 245 million tons of packaging paper and board, 120 million tons of graphic paper, and 55 million tons of other papers were produced in 2017 (VDP 2019). This corresponds to an average use of about 54 kg of paper per person and year, but the distribution for paper is also highly unequal. The annual per capita consumption is 207 kg in North America, 123 kg in Europe, but only 6 kg in Africa (FAO 2019a). Despite its uneven geographies, paper is now firmly established across many aspects of our lives and is thus more than likely to remain a commodity for a long time (Kurlansky 2016).

The European paper industry is a key global player, producing about 90 million tonnes annually or 25 per cent of pulp globally, though this is dwarfed by the USA who produce as much pulp as all of Europe, Canada, Brazil, and Russia combined (FAO 2019a). Just over half of the pulp produced in Europe is from recycled paper, and the rest is from wood. As virgin pulp production is dependent on large volumes of wood, it is concentrated to countries and regions with large, industrially managed forests. European virgin pulp production is thus dominated by a few Nordic countries – Finland and Sweden each produce about 30 per cent of the European virgin pulp (CEPI 2020). The production of paper and board from pulp is more distributed throughout Europe, but Germany dominates with 25 per cent of the production – mainly based on recycled paper – whereas Finland and Sweden each produce about 11 per cent of the European output, most of it in integrated mills producing first pulp and then paper products. While pulp mills are highly integrated and primarily use residual wood to supply the energy to the processes, paper mills do not have the same access to residual wood resources, and they are often dependent on fossil-fuel sources of energy, primarily natural gas. About two-thirds of the fossil carbon dioxide emissions associated with the paper industry, therefore, originate in the production of fine paper and corrugated paperboard for packaging (Moya and Pavel 2018).

While initial environmental concerns related to the paper industry in the 1960s in Europe focused on the local impacts of pulp production, particularly in terms of the production of sulphuric smog and dioxins in watercourses, more recently it has been the vast amount of energy used to process trees into pulp and then paper that have come under scrutiny – paper production is now recognised as one of the most energy-intensive industries in Europe using about 14 per cent of industrial energy (Bergquist and Söderholm 2018). Ever since paper has come into the environmental limelight, attempts have been made to reduce the environmental impact of paper making, to encourage resource efficiencies through the recycling of paper products, and to reduce our consumption of paper. Yet, our paper footprint persists and notions of living without paper tend to find their way into the trash can, or at least the recycling box – take, for example, the idea of the 'paperless office', which has (re)circulated ever since workplace computers became common in the 1990s but has yet to become a reality. In this section, we explore how the decarbonisation of paper has come to be understood and envisioned in the context of previous quests to reduce paper's environmental harm, and how the realities of producing low-carbon paper fare when put to the test, before exploring the prospects for decarbonising this particularly highly energy-intensive sector of the European economy.

Visions

Perhaps because of its long-standing experience of encountering environmental scrutiny, for many in the paper industry new-found concerns about the sector's carbon footprint appear to be relatively easy to address – paper can continue as it is just so long as efficiencies are made and, where necessary, remaining energy needs are met from renewable sources such as biomass residues and renewable electricity. Of all of the sectors examined in this Element, paper then seems to have the easiest path to decarbonisation ahead. Furthermore, a decarbonised economy appears not only straightforward for paper but to offer new opportunities for growth – here paper, and perhaps more importantly, the feedstock on which it relies is seen to have new roles to play through replacing plastic materials, which are both dependent on fossil fuels for their production and highly energy-intensive. Paper's low-carbon economy is primarily then an expansive one. Even where recycling is imagined as central to the future of the paper economy, this is a vision which is based on an ever-expanding role for paper in our society.

Paper Efficiencies

Much is invested in continued energy efficiency to reduce the (fossil) energy demand in the paper sector, for example, the IEA states that '[r]aising the energy efficiency of pulp and paper production is one of the key strategies to decarbonise the sector' (IEA 2020b). Ever since the oil crises in 1970s, pulp mill owners and specialised engineering firms have worked to develop processes and technological equipment that are more energy-efficient and less dependent on foreign supplies of fossil fuels with some success: despite a global increase in paper production of 25 per cent since 2000, energy demand in the sector rose by only 5 per cent, indicating a reduction of 16 per cent in energy intensity in the sector (IEA 2020b). In addition to efficiency measures, fuel switching has also been part of the drive to decarbonise the sector. In Europe, the paper industry has increased its use of biomass significantly while decreasing the use of fuel oil and coal – increasing the share of bioenergy from 44 per cent to 59 per cent of total primary energy consumption from 1991 to 2018 (CEPI 2020). Further, there has been a sustained effort at pulp mills to make use of internally available 'waste' residues as fuels, the largest of which is black liquor – the liquid containing the non-fibre parts of the wood which are separated from the cellulose fibres in the pulping process – which is combusted in the recovery boiler and supplies most of the energy to modern pulp mills.

The drying processes in paper mills are high consumers of heat, the demand for which is primarily met through the use of natural gas, as well as some oil and coal. Paper drying represents up to 70 per cent of the fossil fuel demand in the sector (CEPI 2020). Visions for decarbonising paper mills through improved efficiency measures therefore focus on new and improved drying technologies. These include efficient pressing technologies and innovations such as microwave heating which enables fossil fuels to be switched for (renewable) electricity and simultaneously reduces energy demand. Evidence suggests that microwave heating could reduce 'the dryer energy consumption by 12% by increasing the temperature and drying efficiency' (Moya and Pavel 2018: 39). Despite having been tested and developed for years, these breakthrough technologies have not diffused within the sector. It is likely to take time before they do, given that it requires reconfiguring significant parts of the production processes – a type of change few actors are willing to lead in this risk-averse industry (Wesseling et al. 2017).

Visions for efficiency improvements are almost always combined with the idea that the fossil fuels used in the processes must be substituted for biofuels or other forms of renewable energy, for example, electrified heating and drying

processes running on renewable electricity. CEPI – the European trade association representing the paper industry on the continent – in their roadmap for
2050 aim for a reduction of 80 per cent of GHG emissions by 2050 and argue
that the two of the largest potentials for decarbonising the industry internally are
energy efficiency improvements and fuel switch measures (CEPI 2011). While
most fossil fuel use at pulp mills has been substituted with biofuels, a few key
processes have, for different reasons, remained dependent on oil for a long time.
One of the hardest nuts to crack has been how to decarbonise the lime kiln,
a piece of equipment that is crucial for chemically regenerating the lime needed
in the pulping process. This requires high temperatures properly distributed
along the kiln and thus high-quality fuels.

Towards a Paper-Based Economy?

Beyond industry-led visions for a more resource and efficient sector, visions for
the role of paper in decarbonisation extend to its role in the economy as a whole.
A vision that has rapidly grown in popularity in the past two decades – despite
early origins in the 1980s – is the idea of converting pulp mills to forest
biorefineries (Söderholm and Lundmark 2009). The vision portrays the future
of pulp mills as advanced processing units that use wood to produce a wide
range of products beyond conventional pulp and paper, including bio-based
plastics and complex chemicals, new types of textile fibres, and biofuels to be
used in cars or other vehicles (Bauer et al. 2017). Although the biorefinery
vision is varied, it can be divided into two main ideas: in the first, the primary
output of pulping processes – wood cellulose fibres – are repurposed for new
applications; in the second, by-products, side streams, and residues from the
pulp-making process are captured for the production of new products. If in
the second vision, such new outputs remain essentially a sideline to the main
economy of papermaking, in the former the use of paper is itself reduced to
make space for new forms of economic activity.

   The potential role of the pulp and paper industry in the bioeconomy has been
central to the vision of the forest biorefinery – as promoted by the EU, OECD,
and other policy organisations (de Besi and McCormick 2015). These visions
connect important political discourses on renewable energy, rural development,
and green industrial growth to promote the use of domestic natural resources for
the production of biofuels and other bioproducts (Befort 2020). The policy
visions and support for developing production of other advanced materials and
products has however been weaker. The European pulp and paper industry has
thus had different drivers to push the vision of developing biorefineries: their
access to and knowledge of processing large volumes of bio-based raw

materials, regulations mandating the use of biofuels, as well as changes in markets and consumer behaviour away from traditional products (Brunnhofer et al. 2020).

Industry actors also promote this vision, especially the large Scandinavian firms which own or have access to forest raw materials – five of the ten largest firms in the European pulp and paper industry are indeed Scandinavian. The Finnish firm Metsä, one of the largest forest industry groups in the world, decided on upgrading their pulp mill at Äänekoski not only to make it 'the largest wood processing unit in the northern hemisphere' but also to move away from the traditional focus on producing pulp and instead make it a 'bioproduct mill' capable of producing multiple outputs such as biogas and biocomposites (Metsä Fibre n.d.). The mill was also designed to run development and demon-stration projects to test new processes for textile fibres and fertilisers, which – if successful – can be implemented in full scale later. The old Swedish firm SCA, which owns both forests and pulp mills, is planning a biorefinery for large-scale production of biofuels for cars and vehicles when expanding one of their pulp mills in Sweden. The biorefinery will use solid residues such as wood shavings and bark as well as black liquor from the pulping process. There are, however, also examples of initiatives outside the Scandinavian region, such as the new biorefinery being developed by the Finnish firm UPM in connection to the Leuna chemical cluster in Germany, where they will produce biochemicals by directly substituting fossil ones used in the production of PET plastics as well as bio-based filler materials, which can also be used in plastics and rubbers.

Renewing Recycling

Finally, recycling is a strong vision in the pulp and paper industry as evident from the use of 'recycled' as one of the keywords in the slogan for CEPI: 'renewable, recycled, responsible' (CEPI n.d.). The European industry today produces more paper from recycled material than from virgin materials. The process for making new pulp out of old paper is more efficient than making virgin pulp and thus has the potential to contribute to decarbonisation – if the energy used is renewable. The European Paper Recycling Council on their homepage proudly states that 'Europe is the paper recycling champion!' with a recycling rate of 72 per cent in 2017 – compared to 66 per cent in North America and 58 per cent totally in the world. Driven by both public concern and European regulations, the collection of paper has been established throughout the EU and is already fairly efficient, for example, when compared to plastics, which has much lower recycling rates. The EU packaging and packaging waste directive has the most ambitious targets for paper and board packaging recycling, stating that in 2025 75 per cent of all paper and board packaging should be recycled and that this rate should increase to 85 per cent by 2030. This can be compared to the targets for plastics and aluminium, which are 50 per cent in 2025, to be increased to 55 per cent and 60 per cent, respectively, by 2030. As packaging is the largest demand category for paper in the EU, this shows that there is a large potential for the production of recycled papers, and today they can also be used for many applications. However, the recycling vision is at the same time limited to certain pulp and paper value chains – few are proposing recycling schemes for used napkins and diapers. Such sanitary and household paper products make up about 10 per cent of total paper consumption in Europe (CEPI 2020), which thus sets a limit on the products which are available for recycling, unless consumers move away from their preference for disposable products of this type and embrace the use of ones which can be washed and reused many times.

Realities

Paper's realities may at first hand seem more decarbonised than many of the other sectors explored in this Element. With a history of implementing efficiency measures behind it and ambitions emerging to play a larger role in the low-carbon economy, paper may once again be reinventing itself as the material of the future. At the same time, we find that as these visions are translated, key pinch points are emerging that raise questions as to whether they can indeed be fulfilled by an ever more global industry.

Making Efficiencies

Since the 1970s, pulp mills across Europe have improved their energy efficiency and reduced their energy and carbon intensity. Whereas environmental regulation pushed the development of processes which reduced emissions of sulphur and other local pollutants, efficiency improvements have been driven largely by increasing energy prices following the energy crises of the 1970s and the industry fearing increasing competition for their raw materials in Scandinavia (Bergquist and Söderholm 2018). Through continuous upgrades and retrofits, the boilers, evaporators, and other process equipment have been exchanged for more modern equipment with higher capacities and levels of efficiency. Slowly but surely, pulp mills and integrated pulp and paper mills have thus been able to reduce and remove boilers and heaters running on coal, oil, and gas and replace them primarily with energy from the recovery boiler. Significant decarbonisation has thus been achieved, but a large part of this has not been driven directly by climate policy (Lindmark et al. 2011).

With these improvements undertaken, attention has turned to removing the last link to fossil-fuel use in chemical pulp mills: to decarbonise the lime kilns. Lime kilns are crucial parts of chemical recovery – a series of processes which enable the recirculation and reuse of most chemicals used in the pulping process – at chemical pulp mills and have been difficult to decarbonise due to their technical specifications. Their central role in the pulp mill has also made them difficult to experiment with – without an operating lime kiln the pulp mill has to shut down, which makes new solutions a great risk for fear of losing production and hence profit. Yet, some examples can be found where this risk has been mitigated. A case in point is SCA, one of the largest integrated wood products and pulp and paper firms which had strategically aimed to reduce their environmental impact, including carbon dioxide emissions in the 2000s. When deciding to upgrade the lime kiln at their pulp mill Munksund in central Sweden in 2009, they decided to aim for a fully biofueled lime kiln. Together with the specialised technology developer and engineering firm Andritz they developed and installed a new lime kiln in 2011, which runs on wood powder from one of the pellet production units in the company. Andritz were able to overcome technological difficulties of using solid fuel by learning from decades of development of other powder burners – some of which had been used to partially supply energy to other lime kilns – to reach 100 per cent biofuel utilisation in the lime kiln. Following this, Valmet – a competitor to Andritz – also developed a similar solution, which SCA then went on to install in another pulp mill a few years later. Now both firms – which are two of the largest technology suppliers to the pulp and paper industry in the world – offer this as a standard option for pulp mills when retrofitting or upgrading. Other forms of innovation are also emerging for contexts where access to wood powder is not possible; for example, at the previously mentioned Äänekoski mill in Finland, the kiln successfully runs on gas from a bark gasifier.

As the lifetime of many of the large and central pieces of equipment such as recovery boilers and paper machines is very long and the investments very large – investment cycles are usually 20 years –meaning that only one or two more major investment opportunities remain until 2050. Continued improvements in efficiencies are thus likely to be adopted by the industry but will not suffice to remove the remaining GHG emissions. An industry roadmap expects that getting below 50–60 per cent reductions by 2050 requires breakthrough technologies to be developed by 2030 and applied in coming investment cycles thereafter (CEPI 2011). As several of these breakthrough technologies – especially for paper-making – rely on electrifying the processes instead of directly using fuels the industry relies on a decarbonised electricity system.

Fibre Economies

Visions for increasing the recycling of paper and for generating new kinds of economy are becoming entwined as the industry is increasingly positioning itself not as a producer of paper products per se, but of fibre. This shift has led not only to those within the pulp and paper sector seeking new markets for their products, such as textiles, but also paper recycling companies recognising their opportunities to recycle textiles, of which many are also cellulose fibres. While the textile and fashion industry has become notorious for its use of resources and low capacity for recycling, several established firms in the pulp and paper industry – or new firms with their knowledge base in the industry – have found their knowledge applicable to a new domain in dire need of new solutions. In the past few years, recycling of textile fibres has thus been pioneered by large firms such as Södra (Sweden), which feeds cotton fabrics into their OnceMore process, mixing them with wood to produce pulp which can then be used for new textile fibre. Lenzing (Austria), a major producer of lyocell fibres, has developed a process called Refibra in which they mix cotton from used textiles with wood to produce new lyocell fibres. A firm that has taken it one step further is the Swedish entrepreneurial firm Renewcell, which in an old pulp mill has started up production of Circulose, a pulp based completely on recycled textiles. These examples clearly show how decarbonisation efforts – in this case through circulating and recycling materials – are creating new connections across traditional industrial boundaries and how existing knowledge bases can make important contributions for developing new solutions.

Such boundaries are also becoming blurred when it comes to plastics. Although paper and plastics are competing materials – for example, in packaging solutions – they can sometimes also merge into one material. A biocomposite is a material consisting of two (or more) mixed materials, of which at least one is biobased. The mixing of fibres and plastics increases the strength and decreases the weight, factors which have contributed to their use in cars and other applications, yet they have still remained a niche category of materials (Holmes 2019). The Finnish firm Stora Enso has developed a biocomposite called Durasense in which wood and cellulose fibres from their pulp production are mixed with a plastic. The development came out of a need to revive a mill which had shut down a large part of the production but coincided with the increasing interest in finding alternatives to plastics in many applications. Together with local collaborators, Stora Enso developed, tested, and marketed the new material, aiming to identify markets where consumers could see and make sense of its bio-based content. The biocomposites allow for substituting up to half of the plastic with fibres from wood, thus reducing the need for virgin fossil-based plastics. As the fibres also provide new structural properties, it allows for use with recycled plastics which would otherwise not be of high enough quality. The downside is of course that as it is a mixed material it is very difficult – if not impossible – to recycle at the end of life.

The drivers for the development of new processes, products, and materials are however not just sustainability concerns. As most of the markets and industries described, the pulp and paper industry has become increasingly globalised over many decades and international trade has increased. The growing global competition from production in countries such as Brazil and China has contributed to the pressure on actors from old industrialised regions for reinvention of their businesses and outputs (Novotny and Nuur 2013). While traditional European firms have developed and built value chains for new types of products on local networks – as in the case of Durasense mentioned earlier – many of them have also invested in new production capacity in South America during the past 20 years. Simultaneously, they are thus both resisting the global competition and contributing to it. To what degree this contributes to diffusing new solutions for decarbonising the industry or whether the increasing price competition leads to decreasing opportunities for innovative investments remains to be seen.

Prospects

The prospects for paper in a low-carbon future are intricately linked to the wider decarbonisation of the economy and the ways in which alternative fibres and materials, particularly plastic, come to be viewed. If, for example, the use of plastics and synthetic fibres continues to be questioned by both consumers and policymakers, paper may come to substitute not only for packaging but for a range of products from agricultural plastics to single-use items of many kinds. While some of these novel applications and products – especially those close to consumers – may well be developed and marketed by small, entrepreneurial firms, it is likely that the fundamental development of new types of fibres and production processes will remain within the domain of the large actors that dominate the industry today and have done so for decades. At the same time, such actors are coming to the fore as they offer new possibilities for the realisation of the circular economy, particularly when it comes to the challenge of textiles. Rather than being dependent on the *removal* of existing incumbent actors, it appears as if the decarbonisation of the paper sector is tied to how incumbent interests come to view their product in the context of the low-carbon transition. Early signs suggest that paper has been rather good at reinventing itself, away from a focus on its end products to instead considering itself as a sector that can both generate materials for a variety of uses and provide an essential part of the emerging circular and bio-based economy.

A decarbonised pulp and paper industry is, however, dependent on a decarbonised energy and especially electricity system. While the industry has contributed to this through its adoption of combined heat and power production, the prospects for increasing this production are limited if natural gas is to be substituted at paper mills in continental Europe and the virgin pulp mills in northern Europe maximise the use of residues for material outputs instead of energy production. The pulp and paper industry is thus likely to be increasingly dependent on purchased electrical power. This will increase electricity demand and add pressure on a power system that also must meet increasing demands for renewable electricity for homes, mobility, and other industries. How and by whom such new demands should be met and paid for remains a contentious issue, as the dependency of high emission sectors of the economy such as paper raises the possibility that the balance between consumers and industries in meeting these costs should be redrawn (Fischer et al. 2016).

Parallel to delivering low-carbon solutions, it will remain paramount that other environmental values remain respected in a future with more pressure on forests to produce paper and other types of fibres. Although the economic value of forests managed to be as productive as possible is unequivocal, there is a growing contestation around the value they actually provide as carbon sinks and ecosystem service providers, leading to increasing pressure on forest management (Pohjanmies et al. 2017). Although afforestation and reforestation are often regarded as important measures to mitigate and reduce the effects of climate change, planted forests seem to provide less of both of these services. As natural environments are under increasing pressure from all directions, forests and oceans are seen as the main reserves of biodiversity. Managed forests have typically been planted with single or few species, leading to a low biodiversity not only among the trees but also other plants, insects, and animals that inhabit the forests. Although large parts of northern Europe remain forested, there is concern about their ecological value and increased pressure for the adoption new forest management practices. The strongest drivers for such shifts are, however, socio-cultural, as forests are important for creating identities and forming a sense of connection to nature for many people (Aggestam et al. 2020). For the pulp and paper industry to retain its credibility as a low-carbon industry and as a critical part of a sustainable bioeconomy, it will become increasingly important to show how it manages these competing pressures and delivers low-carbon solutions as well as ecological value.

5 Meat

In 2003, bio-artists Oron Catts and Ionat Zurr organised the exhibition 'Disembodied cuisine' at the international biological art exhibition *L'art Biotech* in Nantes, France. As part of this exhibition, the artists took some cells from live frogs and grew them over a polymer fibre base until they had multiplied into small portions of cultured (lab-grown) frog steak. At the end of a three-month growth period the 'semi-living' frog steak was cooked and eaten (The Tissue Culture and Art Project 2021). The frog steak may have held little immediate promise from a commercial perspective, not least because of its un-meat-like qualities – it had the texture of 'jellied fabric' according to the artists (Catts and Zurr 2004). It was, however, an early iteration of an emerging cultured meat industry, highlighting the ethical, cultural, financial, and environmental debates that have accompanied discussions around meat production and consumption in recent years.

Questions of how we choose what (not) to eat are becoming more pertinent, in all their complexities, as recognition of the impact of our food production and consumption on the climate is increasing. The issue of meat is partly one of the meat cultures: grounded in cultural narratives around how individuals and societies distinguish between what is deemed suitable and desirable for con-sumption and what is not. The growing awareness of the environmental impact of meat production has added another layer to this debate. To understand the problem of meat and the potential of low-carbon alternatives we thus need to understand what makes meat desirable and how alternatives either change or fulfil these desires. This does not, however, mean that there is no need to pay attention to the economic, political, regulatory, or technological dimensions of meat production and consumption. Indeed, these different dimensions are all deeply intertwined and vary across time and space. The average person today consumes twice as much meat per year (43 kg in 2012) as they did two generations ago. Yet, meat consumption is greatly stratified – ranging between 62 and 116 kg per person per year in OECD countries to as little as 10 kg per person per year in some African countries (Ritchie and Roser 2019). This growth in consumption has been fuelled by a rapid increase in global meat production over the past 50 years (Ritchie and Roser 2019). The world now produces over 320 Mt of meat per year, four times more than it used to produce 50 years ago (OECD and FAO 2016). Asia is by far the largest meat-producing world region accounting for 40–45 per cent of global meat production, while Europe and North America, world leaders in the 1960s, occupy the second and third place, respectively (Ritchie and Roser 2019).

Although meat production is a global business, control of the global meat industry is extremely concentrated. In a process that started 40 years ago and accelerated in the 2000s, transnational corporations have come to control almost every stage of the value chain. Cargill is a prime example, being simultaneously a chief supplier of grain, the world's second biggest feed manufacturer and the third biggest meat processor in terms of sales (Heinrich-Böll-Stiftung et al. 2017). The political economy of meat has numerous environmental and social consequences. More than half of the global GHG emissions attributed to food (26 per cent of total GHG emissions) come from animal products, and half of all farmed animal emissions come from beef and lamb (Poore and Nemecek 2018; Weis 2015). Beyond carbon, the environmental impacts from the meat industry are extremely complex, and include biodiversity loss, land use change, and water pollution (Clark and Tilman 2017). There is also the challenge of nutritional waste emerging from using land to cultivate industrial monocultures for livestock feed instead of human consumption, thus exacerbating instead of alleviating hunger (Weis 2015).

The realisation that the current political economy of meat is not only unsustainable but also pushes crucial planetary boundaries (Willett et al. 2019) has led to calls for (radical) systemic change from various societal actors, including civil society organisations, intergovernmental bodies, industry, and individual citizens. Yet, the way change is envisaged differs among these actors, which in combination with the current political and socio-economic realities, and geographical and cultural variations, carries important implications about the prospects for meat in a decarbonised world.

Visions

What it is that meat is envisioned to become in a decarbonised world varies according to the assumptions made about what needs to change, how change is envisaged, and who should drive that change. On the one hand there is a vision that meat as an *idea* can be retained, albeit that it needs to be produced differently. On the other hand, we find a vision for a *meatless* society, where meat is removed not only from our patterns of consumption but also from our cultures and identities. In each case, visions which are reformist, that is, which take the current world order as a given and aim to improve specific elements within it and which are transformative, that is, where the intention is one of challenging the current world order with its existing underlying power relationships and institutions, can be found.

Making Meat Differently

For many, meat remains a central component of future consumption practices in a decarbonised world such that the need to address its carbon footprint focuses on producing it differently either as a result of technological innovations or as a result of rethinking the ways in which supply chains are organised.

There are numerous versions of this vision to be found in its *reformist expression*, where innovations in the ways in which meat is produced or substituted by products with meat-like qualities are considered the way forward while doing little to challenge the role of meat within our food cultures. As perhaps is to be expected, one proponent is the livestock industry as it comes to recognise the need to align itself with a low-carbon world (e.g. NFU 2019). Smart agriculture based on efficiency principles in terms of natural resource use, waste, and fossil fuel for transport and refrigeration is proposed by inter-governmental bodies and committees as the means through which carbon can be removed from the meat supply chain (UNEP 2016). These include propositions around more effective use of ecosystem services, better-feed conversion, higher nutrient efficiency along the supply chain, and reduction of food losses and food waste. At an experimental phase are alternatives that aim to *change the gut microbiome* of cows in order to produce less methane while digesting food. In New Zealand, for example, cows have been injected with a substance that targets microbe species. If successful, this vaccine developed by AgResearch is intended to be used for other animals as well. At the moment, however, there is lack of definite proof that this vaccine indeed cuts the amount of methane produced by cows (Watts 2019).

A second subset of visions, which are also reformist in orientation, centre on alternative ways of sourcing animal protein. The promotion of insects as an alternative source of animal-based protein is one example, while cultured meat is another, albeit currently at a prototype phase. Cultured meat is grown in vitro from animal-derived stem cells using a growth medium, and as such, it is biologically equivalent to meat but not harvested from live animals. The 'first wave' of the development of cultured meat was primarily driven by university laboratories (sometimes in collaboration with industry). Stephens et al. (2019) neatly describe how a 2013 press conference – where the first laboratory-grown burger was cooked – was key to shaping the emergent vision of cultured meat. By staging the public eating of this burger, cultured meat asserted both its 'realness' as food and its potential in delivering environmental, human health, and animal welfare benefits. Furthermore, the event enabled this nascent industry to bring 'a new aesthetic to the field, focused on style, slickness, and confidence' (Stephens et al. 2019: 4). This new aesthetic bought forth a shift in how this vision was to be realised. Since 2013 start-up companies have become central to the sustenance and realisation of this vision, supported by circuits of venture capital (Froggatt and Wellesley 2019). It is estimated that the value of the global cultured-meat market could reach \$94 billion by 2030

(Research and Markets 2021), although as we explore in the next section, questions remain around the promise and reality of cultured meat.

In contrast to either a focus on process efficiency or cultured meat, both of which remain tied into global circuits of capital and technology, the *transformative expression* of this vision is associated with the development of short food supply chains initiatives and platforms that aim to support local economies and ethical supply chains. These visions seek to undo the carbon content of meat through challenging its political economy – attempting to (re)connect consumers with producers, making visible the different human and non-human elements of the networks that supply our food and encouraging the development of more caring relationships between them. At the heart of this vision are numerous actors, often rooted in social movements, that promote small-scale, geographically specific, and directly marketed foods grown in an ecologically sustainable manner. One such example is the Open Food Network, a global network of people and organisations trying to build a new food system. Founded in 2012 in Australia it has evolved into a locally led international community across the globe. Its flagship project is the development of an open source software platform used by farmers to set up their own online stores, collaborate and sell together. According to the network this has led to the creation of food collectives and given stallholders more secure sales.

Going without Meat

Rather than seeking technological solutions, a second set of visions for decarbonising meat brings to the fore the nature of our demand for meat and the degree to which we can go without – from meat reduction to a switch to vegetarian and vegan diets. This vision is primarily driven by social movements, consumer groups, and individual ethics, although producers of meat substitutes are also important players.

Today about 18 per cent of the global population are considered vegetarian (Leahy et al. 2010). While the first vegetarian societies were established in the middle of the nineteenth century (Jallinoja et al. 2018), there has been a sharp increase in vegans and vegetarians in many Western countries in recent years: in the United States the number of vegans grew 600 times between 2014 and 2017, counting 19.6 million people (The Vegan Society 2019). Similarly, the number of vegans in the United Kingdom quadrupled between 2014 and 2019, and it is projected that vegans and vegetarians will make about a quarter of the British population by 2025 (The Vegan Society 2019). In its transformative expression, veganism is supported by multiple narratives and (dis)connections to meat culture and characterised by a strong moral and ethical stance. The parts of the vegan movement that were most visible in European countries in the 1980s and 1990s were often associated with counter-cultural movements and radical environmental protest, eco-centrism, and post-materialistic values, alongside the promotion of a philosophical worldview that emphasises a more egalitarian relationship between human and non-human animals (Jallinoja et al. 2018). In recent years, however, there are some indications that the growth in veganism has been accompanied by a shift in concerns away from animal welfare, to the climate and environmental impacts of animal agriculture (Hancox 2018).

However, being meat-free is also an individual, 'do-it-yourself', form of activism, reliant on individual lifestyle change. And it is this individualised form – that does not require the consistent alignment between all of someone's actions and values – that has gained the most traction in recent years, resonating with the high value placed on consumer choice and individualism in Western societies (Jallinoja et al. 2018). This reformist expression of being meat-free is often referred to as 'plant-based' or 'flexitarian', indicating a diet that consists primarily of plant-based products which may contain some meat or other forms of animal protein. These labels can appear less threatening to food-based cultural identities compared to the term vegan and its overt political connotations (Judge and Wilson 2015). In this reformist expression, various flexible solutions have emerged for reducing, but not abolishing, meat consumption. These interventions such as 'meatless Mondays' promote a reduced-meat diet for environmental, but also increasingly health, concerns. The idea of meatless Mondays was first introduced during the First World War by the U.S. Food and Drug Administration in order to reduce the consumption of key staples to aid the war and was reintroduced by President Roosevelt during the Second World War (Mullendore and Lutz 1941). Since 2003, it has grown into a global movement supported by hospitals, schools, and individuals around the world. The shift to a reduced-meat diet is increasingly recommended by international organisations, such as the International Resource Panel Working Group on Food Systems and Natural Resources and the EAT Forum (Willett et al. 2019).

There are, however, overlaps between the two visions. In particular, the promotion of vegetarianism or veganism often goes hand in hand with the promotion of meat substitutes. While some vegetarians and vegans reject the idea that plant-based meals should mimic meat, the recent wave of meat substitutes fits the reformist version of this vision: promoting vegetarian alternatives to meat-eaters who wish to reduce their consumption of animal-based protein rather than forego it all together. Such substitutes, especially in the form of *meat analogue*s – that is, products that proximate certain aesthetic qualities and chemical characteristics of specific types of meat (Joshi and Kumar 2015) – straddle the boundary between the two visions. Meat analogues are made from plant-based ingredients and are intended to provide an alternative to those who want to reduce meat consumption as well as give more diversity in vegetarian choices. In the Western world, meat analogues started to develop in the early 1960s, while products such as soy and tempeh have been consumed in Asia for centuries (Wild et al. 2014). Today, the popularity of meat analogues is increasing, particularly as a result of advancing technologies in creating a fibrous texture from plants and tastes that are similar to meat. Experts expect that genetic engineering can enhance the quality of plant-based food products further, thus contributing to a larger uptake of these products in the market (Joshi and Kumar 2015). While such products emphasise their non-meatlike qualities in order to set them apart, they do not reject the idea of meat altogether. Not only do such products increasingly seek to mimic the textures, flavours, and colours of meat, but also to highlight the presence of favourable nutrients, especially protein. Rather than setting meat substitutes apart, according to some experts this focus on protein can thus serve to break down the boundary between animal and non-animal foods by emphasising their 'sameness', thus aiming to make the transition easier (Sexton et al. 2019).

Realities

These visions confront several realities that shape both the ways in which they come to be structured and understood, as well as the nature and dynamics of their potential to lead us to a decarbonised meat economy.

Reducing the Carbon Footprint of Meat

Reducing the carbon footprint of meat value chains through waste reduction, different feed, and different breeds has potential but these strategies alone are insufficient to bring us to a decarbonised future. For example, it is estimated that around 14.5 per cent of meat is wasted at the retail and consumption stage and saving this loss can reduce GHG emissions by leading to less meat production in the future (FAO 2011). However, it is unclear what the exact contribution to climate change would be from this form of intervention. Changing animal feed and animal breeds could lead to GHG emissions reduction between 10 per cent and 30 per cent but not without side effects (Aan den Toorn et al. 2018). For example, reducing methanogens could prove toxic to cattle, while we know little about what this means for other animals. And the possibility of developing breeds that produce less methane could create ruminants which suffer from adverse effects in their digestive system (Aan den Toorn et al. 2018).

Politically, carbon reduction measures in the meat economy are also not fully supported momentarily. For example, the Common Agricultural Policy (CAP) hinders decarbonisation efforts as it is still centrally focused on productivity-based measures that promote the increased intensification of food production. Studies show that the CAP has very limited capacity to deliver on climate action because it lacks instruments to address emissions from livestock production and those resulting from imported feedstock from overseas (Pe'er et al. 2017). In addition, while the CAP supports organic farming and more environmentally sensitive agricultural methods, it simultaneously incentivises intensification and offers disproportionate support for meat and dairy products (Pe'er et al. 2017). The European Commission tried to address some of the CAP's negative environmental (and by extension climate) impacts by introducing green payments to farmers in 2013. This mechanism was expected to enhance the environmental performance of CAP by rewarding farmers to provide environmental public goods. However, a report by the European Commission (2018c) found that the new payment scheme lacks clear and ambitious climate targets. For example, there are no compulsory measures for emission reductions from livestock, only optional ones. The report concludes that '*the CAP measures are therefore not relevant to a significant proportion of the EU's climate mitigation needs*'. (European Commission 2018c: 39; emphasis added). While some commentators see rather little evidence of meaningful ongoing or future changes to the CAP that would enable decarbonisation (Pe'er et al. 2017, 2019), others see a game-changing potential of the EU's Farm to Fork Strategy now being implemented as part of the Green Deal (Schebesta and Candel 2020).

Removing Meat from the Economy

It appears from the above discussion that removing meat from the economy is necessary in supporting decarbonisation efforts. One important set of realities here that challenges these interventions comes from industry incumbency and the current structure of the meat industry. Industry incumbents can have a significant influence on innovation success, especially when market power is concentrated (as in meat) and through the influence of public regulation and discourse (Smink et al. 2015). As a result, the impact of technological alternatives, and meat analogues in particular, can go in two directions. On the one hand, they can pose a threat to conventional supply chains by shifting consumers away from conventional meat with negative implications for meat industry incumbents. On the other hand, meat analogues offer an opportunity to the meat industry to diversify and reduce future risks. Early funding for analogues – in particular, cultured meat – often came from alternative sources of finance, including crowdfunding and venture capital firms who banked on cultured meat's potential to 'disrupt' the existing food system (Stephens et al. 2019). However, in recent years many of the meat giants have come to embrace meat analogues. Examples include meat processing company Tyson foods, with investments in Memphis Meats and Beyond Meat, and Unilever, with investments in the Plant Meat Matters consortium and the Vegetarian Butcher (Froggatt and Wellesley 2019). The explanation offered by the Chief Sustainability Officer at Tyson food is particularly insightful: 'we don't want to be disrupted . . . We want to be part of the disruption' (Koning Beals 2018). It is important to emphasise, however, that there are currently no cultured meat products on the market. Instead, their growing importance in envisioning a low-carbon meat future – and the ability to attract increasing sums of investment – is largely premised on a set of promissory narratives, centred on what it is that cultured meat will achieve once it is on the market and presenting it as the logical solution to meat's multiple problems (Sexton et al. 2019).

The realities of cultural incumbency also matter and play a role in resisting the introduction of new narratives. Cultural incumbency can create resistance to changes that threaten lifestyles, identities, and traditions. In many countries in the Global North products of animal origin are often deemed superior to plant foods and cereals, a pattern that has not changed since it was first studied in the 1970s (Schösler et al. 2012). Throughout history, complex societies made use of meat to establish social distinctions of wealth and status, as well as to unify people through the symbolic manipulation of animals in ritual (deFrance 2009). In modern times, celebratory meals such as during Christmas, Easter, and Thanksgiving are associated with particular types of meat cooking and eating. However, in current Western diets, meat is of course not restricted to special meals, and its consumption is heavily routinised through its incorporation in everyday meals. Addressing meat consumption will mean attending both to meat's special status and the routine forms of consumption that are the result of industrialisation and expansion of the meat industry (Schösler et al. 2012).

The introduction of a novel innovation, such as meat analogues, thus requires a process of 'sense-making' – a process through which meaning is given to an innovation or practice and which tries to establish its desirability. This is particularly relevant in relation to cultured meat, as it has not always been clear where this fits in the animal/non-animal dichotomy. This has resulted in an inherent paradox in the way in which it has been presented: as both ontologically similar and different to 'conventional' meat (Stephens et al. 2019). As the number of stakeholders involved in the development of cultured meat (and other meat analogues) has grown, this process of sense-making has become entangled in competing values over what a protein food system should look like and what (in)tangible services it should deliver (Sexton et al. 2019). Equally, this process of sense-making is highly differentiated across social groups. A case in point here is the gendered consumption of meat. The idea that 'real men eat meat' is attributed to the time of hunter gatherers and men participation in hunting large game and subsequent meat-sharing activities, gaining them a reputation of being tough and daring (Rothgerber 2013). Although advances in gender equality and a more shared commitment to domestic activities by men challenge this attitude, women continue to be more likely to reduce their meat consumption than men, and groups that attach traditional roles to men and women are more resistant to replacing or reducing meat consumption than others (Hancox 2018).

Given these economic and cultural incumbencies, state actors are often at the forefront of seeking to enable change. While some focus on providing knowledge to individual consumers to change to their diet, maintaining the idea that food remains a matter of individual choice (Sexton et al. 2019), others seek out approaches that actively support technological innovation. For example, in the Netherlands, governmental actors support the innovation in meat substitutes, partly because it is an opportunity to respond to growing public pressure without directly challenging the meat sector. In general, the promotion of innovation is politically more feasible than the promotion of reducing consumption or decreasing production capacity of established sectors (Tziva et al. 2020). Public procurement can also play a role in protecting the vegetarian niches and allowing them to grow. Universities and schools, for instance, can offer more if not exclusive vegetarian options. Public procurement criteria for food across the EU now stipulate that there should be an increased offer in plant-based menus by introducing weekly vegetarian days and plant-based proteins in catering services (European Commission 2019a).

However, in other areas, states and their regulatory systems have acted in ways that may hamper the introduction of alternative products. In some places, contestation over meat analogues has resulted in the introduction of legislation that prohibits the use of the label 'meat' for food that does not originate from conventional (slaughtered) animals. The use of genetic modification in some cultured meat products also remains a source of regulatory uncertainty within the EU. Even if cultured meat companies seek to comply with current regulations, it is highly like that relevant regulations will change to deal with the novel challenges cultured meats poses (e.g. regarding traceability), which may delay the introduction of such products in Europe (Stephens et al. 2019). The emergence of alternatives thus needs to be accompanied by changes that challenge existing production systems.

Prospects

Which of the visions outlined earlier are more likely to gain track and become actualised in the context of the aforementioned realities? To a certain extent all visions co-develop rather than compete with one another. The reformist aspects of changing the meat economy all rely on one another in order to gain their own legitimacy and traction. Thus, efficiency in the value chain, reducing meat use, and creating meat alternatives serve to reduce carbon but also to 'lock-in' a new system of lower-carbon meat which may also stop more radical forms of decarbonisation (see also Hoffmann and Bernstein 2020). At the same time, transformative visions for decarbonisation of meat are in a sense also partly dependent on some of the reformist experimentation with meat alternatives. The latter is a means through which they can start to achieve rather radical new kinds of consumption but without moving cultural norms.

Transformative visions require deeper political, economic, and sociocultural changes. Importantly, transformative visions can also institute such changes. Indeed, while there can be no substantial dietary shifts without changing cultures around meat, the shifts that are already taking place are beginning to change these 'meat cultures'. Likewise, different models of organising meat value chains simultaneously demand a shift away from concentrated trans-national supply chains, and in doing so, begin to create this shift.

It is evident that a supportive institutional context would enable transformative visions to take root, accelerate, and spread. Importantly, the aim of the 2020 Green New Deal currently being negotiated for Europe is to establish the objective of the EU being climate neutral by 2050 as part of the European Climate Law as well as to integrate sustainability in all aspects of EU's policies (European Commission 2019b). Such a Green New Deal could potentially disrupt many of the realities underlined earlier in favour of deep transformations. Analysts, however, are sceptical about the ability of the Commission to institute such change as it is constrained by the institutional structure of the EU itself. Such a holistic approach, which is not yet evident (Adler and Wargan 2019), is essential to ensure the ambition of such a program is not watered down. However, without transformative change, there is a risk that decarbonisation of the meat economy will remain limited to technological fixes and efficiency measures. This also has implications for the geographies and power relations embedded in meat consumption and production. One concern is that techno-fixes, including cultured meat, might exacerbate uneven power relations between the Global North and South, with the innovations of Northern corporations undermining local food systems (Sexton et al. 2019). Furthermore, as we know from a long history of environmental governance and failure, these approaches alone are inadequate to achieve the magnitude of change that we need, and to do so in a socially just way, a point to which we return in the conclusions.

6 Milk

With cornflakes for breakfast or in a sandwich for lunch, as a frozen snack to cool down in summer or mixed with chocolate to warm yourself up in winter: there are few types of food that have become quite so prominent in the everyday Western diet as milk and its associated products. Before the late nineteenth century, milk was rarely consumed in liquid form but rather as cheese, butter, or yoghurt in order to preserve it and limit the chance of accidental poisoning. Because of its potential adverse effects, milk has long been held in suspicion and its consumption shunned by more urban and wealthier members of European society (Valenze 2011). From the middle of the nineteenth century onwards, however, milk started to become equated with a healthy life (Atkins 2010). Through the introduction of a host of sanitation measures, politicians and other stakeholders sought to tackle liquid milk's earlier association with the transmission of diseases. Although some conflict over pasteurisation and the commodity's health benefits remained, to a large extent milk came to be associated with positive normative qualities: 'Melk is goed voor elk' (milk is good for everyone) as the slogan used by the Dutch Dairy Federation in the second half of the twentieth century put it. These positive associations were also fostered through the relationship between state and capital. In Sweden, as elsewhere in Europe, milk became the important economic and cultural industry it is today because its ambitions were aligned with that of the governing social democratic state (Jönsson 2005). The elevation of the living standards of the working class was helped by programmes such as free milk in schools. The very structure of the dairy industry, decentralised and rural, also aligned with ideals of increasing employment as well as securing a stable food supply for the country. Over the last century, dairy has transformed from a food that was shunned by elites into a Western icon of both modern nutrition and societal well-being: 'the perfect food' (DuPuis 2002).

Understanding both milk's malleable qualities and the culture(s) through which it has emerged as a key staple in many Western diets is integral to understanding its potential low-carbon pathways. Milk is both a product of culture and a mirror of it: reflecting attitudes towards the countryside, the human body, non-humans, technology, and so much more (e.g. DuPuis 2002; Valenze 2011). Milk is not just natural nor is it fully cultural, instead it is a (set of) product(s) continuously imagined, re-imagined, contested, and transformed (Atkins 2010). Despite varied regional histories, there is one animal that rules them all when it comes to milk production in modern Europe: the noble cow (FAO 2019b). Yet even cow's milk is far from a singular product: only just over 10 per cent of all milk produced in the EU is used to produce drinking milk, with much larger quantities used to produce cheese and butter (Eurostat 2018). As cow's milk came to be associated with a healthy diet through the twentieth century, farmers became required to use economies of scale to produce the 'superabundance' of milk that society had begun to expect and demand (Valenze 2011). As a result of a growth in overall calorie intake and diet composition (IPCC 2019), per capita consumption of milk has grown globally by almost 20 per cent between 1961 and 2013 (Ritchie and Roser 2017). Combined with a growing population, this has ensured that milk production has more than doubled during this period (Ritchie and Roser 2017). While this growing demand for milk has been partly met through increased yields, it has also necessitated more cows. To meet this growth in demand, the number of cattle has increased by more than 50 per cent since 1961 (IPCC 2019). This not only has important implications for the climate, but it has also had a variety of other environmental consequences, including the loss of natural ecosystems and declining biodiversity as well as increased pressure on global freshwater use (IPCC 2019).

Addressing the European decarbonisation challenge for the milk sector may at first glance appear to be relatively straightforward as the milk economy remains primarily regional rather than global in scope. Due to the challenges in transporting liquid milk over both space and time, more than 90 per cent of all milk production is consumed within the regions where it is produced (FAO 2019c). Decarbonising European milk is therefore not subject to some of the challenges related to global value changes and forms of competition found in other sectors addressed in this Element. Yet we find the decarbonisation challenge lies in the interweaving of political, cultural and economic factors, enabled through long-standing institutional support, which has helped it gain a stronghold in the heart of European diets. In the rest of this section, we explore two contrasting low-carbon visions for the dairy sector, their respective realities, and the prospects for removing carbon from our refrigerator shelves.

Visions

Until recently, the climate implications of milk futures have passed largely unnoticed. Mainstream visions for the dairy industry – like all of the sectors addressed in this Element – continue to envisage a continued upward trend in milk production (Figure 5). However, as climate change comes to be

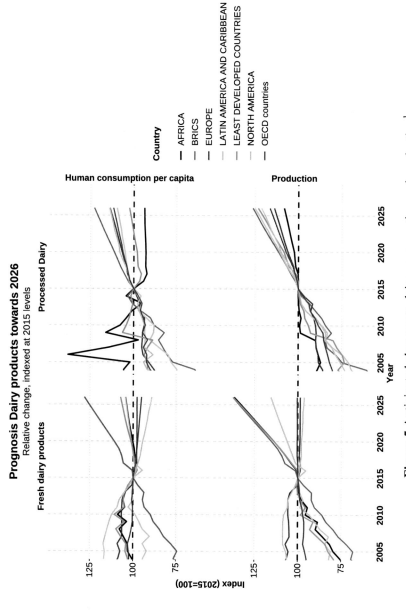

Figure 5 Anticipated changes to dairy consumption and production[1]

Source: OECD and FAO 2016

---

[1] The volatility in processed dairy consumption in Africa appears to be the result of significant fluctuations in the consumption of milk powder. Unfortunately, we have been unable to definitively determine the cause of these fluctuations.

increasingly positioned as a dietary issue reflecting the now well-known association between meat-based diets and carbon emissions (Section 5), milk's carbon futures are increasingly coming into view. As a result, we can identify two broad visions around dairy emerging: one that has emerged through the dairy industry and international actors such as the FAO and OECD, seeking to address dairy's climate impacts while reinforcing its status as part of a healthy diet; while the other brings together environmental activists and scientists and seeks to challenge the levels of dairy consumption in Western diets.

Good Milk Futures

Recognising the need to engage with the climate agenda, major actors in the dairy sector have set out their visions for their role in low-carbon transitions with actors such as Arla, one of the largest dairy companies in the world, committing to reaching 'net-zero carbon' by 2050, while the UK's National Farmers Union seeks to achieve this goal by 2040. Tied into this vision of milk as low-carbon is a continued emphasis on its qualities in delivering a 'good life'. Far from being part of the problem, in this vision the dairy industry positions itself as part of the solution to decarbonising the economy.

To date, the climate story told by the dairy industry has focused on emphasising the improvements made in reducing the emissions per kg milk produced. For example, Dutch dairy company FrieslandCampina sought to make emissions efficiency visible through translating it into a target of 'climate-neutral growth' (increasing production without increasing emissions) for the company. It is thought that emissions intensity can be reduced by a further 50 per cent in Europe and North America by 2050 through efficiency increases and technological innovation (e.g. Hedenus et al. 2014). It is, however, unlikely that emissions can be reduced much further without eliminating the source of much of these emissions: the cow. Production processes used to make fresh milk ready for market are only responsible for a small proportion of emissions. Instead, the vast majority of emissions – about 85 per cent according to Arla (2019c) – come from the farm, in the form of methane and nitrous oxide. As such, as Arla, FrieslandCampina, and others acknowledge, decarbonising the dairy chain is likely to be impossible. Instead, Arla's vision, as well as other visions emergent from the dairy industry, relies heavily on improved land management practices and investing in carbon offsetting programmes in order to achieve the net-zero goal (see Arla 2019c). With these measures in place, Arla was able to declare in an advertising campaign in 2019 'we have the future in our hands – welcome to the dairy of the future' and to launch their first climate-neutral dairy range.

In making the case for milk, both its nutritional properties and socio-economic importance are emphasised. For example, the Food and Agriculture Organization of the United Nations (FAO) together with the Global Dairy Platform (a global industry body for the dairy industry) suggest in their report on the role of the sector in a low-carbon future that 'dairy products are a rich source of essential nutrients that contribute to a healthy and nutritious diet' (FAO and GDP 2018: 6). At the same time, companies such as Arla emphasise how the continuation of the dairy sector is critical for meeting the Sustainable Development Goals, such as Goal 2 – Zero hunger, Goal 3 – Good health and well-being, and Goal 12 – Sustainable consumption (e.g. Arla 2019b). Making milk climate neutral is therefore positioned as a means through which these benefits can continue to be realised while at the same time meeting carbon responsibilities.

Getting Beyond the White Stuff

For other actors, these visions of dairy as part of the solution are difficult to swallow. Alternative visions – promoted by actors including animal and environmental activists, alternative food producers, and some in the science community – suggest instead the need to imagine a future with reduced or no dairy consumption. Long-standing concerns from animal rights activists about the prominence of milk in our diets are now joined by those pointing to its environmental impacts. One case in point has been the development of the 'planetary health diet', advocated by a coalition of 37 scientists from 16 countries brought together in the EAT-Lancet Commission. Its aim was to reach scientific consensus by defining targets for sustainable food production and healthy diets. In their report, the Commission argued that guidelines for dairy consumption in developed nations (especially the United States) are often based on limited evidence, while the optimum amount of dairy consumption remains uncertain (Willett et al. 2019). In arguing that 'a wide range of intakes are compatible with a good health' (Willett et al. 2019: 456), the Lancet report thus directly challenges the vision presented by the dairy industry, which places dairy at the heart of the vision for a good and healthy life. Unlike previous campaigns, these scientific endeavours do not necessarily seek to promote veganism – which is still often seen as socially unfeasible – but instead focus on a shift towards diets with lower levels of dairy consumption than the current average European or North American diet. Climate and environmental scientists have sought to model what impacts such shifts could have, finding, for example, that in 64 per cent of countries the GHG emissions footprint of a 'no dairy' diet was lower than that of a vegetarian diet in which the protein derived from meat is replaced by protein derived from dairy (Kim et al. 2019).

It is not only milk's carbon credentials that are under scrutiny: what is noticeable about this second set of visions is that the need for dietary change in relation to decarbonisation is connected to other concerns around animal welfare and biodiversity, and also seeks to challenge established wisdoms regarding dairy's role in a healthy diet. While in the case of the meat economy, suggested dietary changes include alternative animal products to beef, we find there is limited engagement with animal-based milk alternatives – such as goat milk – which already have niche markets for those with lactose intolerance. Yet as we will explore further in the text, attempts to think beyond and around the cow are now emerging as the realities of how to live without the white stuff come to be put to the test.

Realities

If the politics of milk once revolved around seeking to stabilise its health risks with stakeholders all seeking to 'have their interests protected, or their solutions implemented' (Atkins 2010: xix), today such a politics is being relived through the realities of what it means to decarbonise the milk sector. The visions sketched out earlier are generating diverse forms of intervention, mobilised through distinct actor groups and with profoundly different implications for the future of the sector, such that there is now all to play for in the future of the European milk economy.

Dialling Down Dairy's Carbon Footprint

Farmers, scientists, and other stakeholders from the agricultural sector are primarily seeking to govern milk's carbon qualities by reducing the emissions intensity of the value chain by targeting two key sites: farms and factories. Given that the majority of emissions are to be found 'on farm', this is a critical site for intervention. Of the emissions from livestock, approximately 44 per cent is in the form of methane (Gerber et al. 2013) with much of the remainder being nitrous oxide. Unfortunately, these emissions are also among the hardest to tackle. Interventions include those that try to address reductions in enteric methane (the production of methane by microbes living in cows' guts); reductions in nitrous oxide through manure management; sequestering carbon in pastures; implementation of best animal husbandry and management practices, which would have an effect on most GHGs; and land-use practices that also help sequester carbon. Of these, the most promising tend to be those that try to address enteric methane – which is primarily emitted through cow burps. Feed supplements that reduce the efficiency with which microbes produce methane can potentially deliver methane reductions of up to 30 per cent, although much of the research is still in the early stages. While single solutions are limited in their potential, there are promising indications that in combination they may have the potential to reduce farm-based methane and nitrogen emissions by up to 50 per cent (Aan den Toorn et al. 2021). This, however, still leaves 50 per cent of on-farm emissions unaddressed, requiring some level of 'offsetting' in order to realise carbon neutrality.

The second place where the dairy industry has begun to target emissions is in its processing factories. Here, emissions are related to electricity use and can be readily achieved through efficiency measures and existing technologies such as the use of solar energy, biomass or bioenergy, or other forms of process optimisation (Monforti-Ferrario et al. 2015). Nonetheless, as only a small percentage of all dairy emissions originate from these factories (likely to be in the region of 10 per cent or less), the overall decarbonisation potential is rather small. What is notable about attempts to increase the efficiency of milk's use and to offset the (carbon) impacts of its production is that such interventions usually do not cross the threshold from the sphere of production into the various places in which milk is consumed. This is notable as estimates show that approximately 7.5 per cent of milk is wasted at the retail and consumption stage (FAO 2011). Furthermore, the foodservice sector (e.g. cafes) is a major purchaser of dairy. As the COVID-19 pandemic showed, when consumption in this sector suddenly declines, it can create tremendous wastage upstream in the supply chain (Tatum 2020). Although eliminating wastage could thus theoretically reduce demand for dairy production whilst still maintaining its role in Western diets, the nature of the dairy supply chain makes this a challenging prospect.

From Milk to Mylk: The Emergence and Growth of Plant-Based Alternatives

Rather than making milk more carbon-efficient, a second set of interventions align with visions which see its reduction or removal from our diets as the way forward. One key element here has been the development of 'plant-based' milk alternatives. While such 'plant milks', especially soy milk, have a long history in China, they were not produced on a commercial scale in the United States or Europe until the mid-twentieth century (Mylan et al. 2019). Early iterations of plant-based milk tended to be based on soy, rice, or almond, popular amongst a minority with special dietary needs. Seen as a specialised niche, such plant-based alternatives struggled to demonstrate their necessity in the face of the stable reproduction of milk's dietary qualities. Yet, this has begun to change as milk has come under pressure because of its environmental impacts in the past decade. Although the share of plant-based milks is still relatively small – averaging 5–10 per cent of the market share compared to liquid dairy in Europe and North America (Mylan et al. 2019) – sales of plant-based milks continue to grow. As a result, Mylan et al. (2019) conclude that plant-based milks have gained sufficient momentum and scale to now be on their way to become part of the mainstream in the United Kingdom.

An important explanation for the success of plant-based milks is that these interventions have sought not to specifically target individual behavioural choices made on the grounds of environmental concerns but rather to weave their way into the everyday routines and practices of consumption as a means through which to gain both visibility and shift consumption norms. For example, American soy and almond milk brands understood the importance of being displayed in the refrigerated aisle in supermarkets, next to the cow-based milks. Not only do such aisles attract higher traffic, but it also fosters certain cultural connotations, around the freshness of the product and its interchangeability with dairy-based milks. Oatly, a Swedish oat-milk brand, has produced a Barista Edition, seamlessly enabling the consumption of vegan milky coffees that try to emulate the texture and consistency of non-vegan versions, while also enabling its consumption outside the domestic sphere and sustaining the cultural practice of its main consumer base – relatively young urban people in North American and Northern Europe – going out for a coffee with friends or buying a coffee 'on the go'. Not only are infrastructures thus adapting themselves to the new demand for plant-based products through the proliferation of vegan supermarkets and restaurants, but also through the introduction of plant-based alternatives in already existing (not exclusively vegan) spaces.

Oatly provides further insight into how and why plant-based alternatives may have enjoyed more success than similar products in the meat sector. While Oatly was originally designed as an alternative product for those with specific dietary needs, a company representative explained the brand's success by pointing to its ability to tap into a wider set of desires and concerns: emphasising its planetary stewardship, sustainability, and the fostering of connections to a new type of consumer. Importantly, Oatly has not just focused on individual consumption, but rather sought to overcome inertia by creating a group identity based on not drinking milk. In doing so, the brand has balanced a fine line between emphasising its non-cowness (e.g. through its slogan 'Wow no Cow') and its similarity to regular milk ('It's like milk but made for humans'). Hence, like other producers of plant-based milk, it has conceptualised milk based on its material functions – the provision of milkiness – while simultaneously considering milk not derived from animal glands as superior (Jönsson et al. 2019). Without having to deal with the inefficiencies of cows' 'cumbersome corporeality', proponents argue, milk production can become more resource-efficient, tackling both environmental and animal welfare concerns without sacrificing the functions that milk fulfils (Jönsson et al. 2019).

Yet by integrating itself into already existing spaces and practices, producers of plant-based milk can serve to not only underscore the inefficiencies of cow-milk but also reinforce the perception of milk as a desirable source of nutrition and part of an everyday diet (Jönsson et al. 2019). Indeed, the main reason for developing an oat drink is because it mimics the functionality and cultural connotations of milk (rather than the nutritional profile), enabling it to be easily integrated into already-existing lifestyles. Oatly has *both* positioned itself as an alternative to milk while also pointing to its similarities to dairy, thereby making a switch to oat drink convenient, while reinforcing the central role that milk plays in many Western countries.

Plant-based interventions have not gone unnoticed by the dairy industry, which has responded by contesting the environmental claims of plant-based milk proponents through developing alternative metrics for measuring the climate impact of milk. For example, researchers connected to the Swedish Dairy Association used a new metric – the nutrient density to climate impact (NDCI) index – to conclude that milk provides eight times the nutritional value in relation to its emissions when compared to oat drink (Smedman 2017). However, others have questioned such research, arguing that depending on the value you attribute to an arbitrary variable in the authors' equation, you get different results and only in a certain span does milk come out on top (Scarborough and Rayner 2010). Such contestation does not always damage plant-based alternatives. When Oatly portrayed itself as being similar to milk, but better ('No Milk. No Soy. No Badness'), this was resisted by the Swedish dairy industry who took the company to court over its portrayal of milk. While Oatly lost the case, it has helped to increase the visibility of the brand, 'turning conflict into a marketing device' (Jönsson et al. 2019: 86). Through the involvement of grassroots campaigns, the Oatly case became an opportunity for people to engage in food politics and re-assess their own practices in relation to the foods they consume (Jönsson et al. 2019).

Prospects

Reducing the carbon content of milk has limited potential, leading those in the dairy industry to promote a combination of agricultural innovations for the cow's digestive system and efficiency measures in the processing of milk combined with offsetting schemes as the way to get to 'net zero', despite rising concerns voiced about whether and how carbon can be successfully offset through measures such as forest conservation or the restoration of degraded landscapes. Alternative visions which promote the overall reduction or removal of dairy from (largely Western) diets as the means through which decarbonisation can be achieved are beginning to make some progress, but the extent to which they can fully replace the dairy sector seems partial at best. Furthermore, while plant-based milks are increasingly commonplace in supermarket aisles, alternatives to other dairy products are lagging behind – though the first vegan cheese mongers are now a reality in both the United States and Europe. The problem with milk – and attempts to change dairy consumption practices – is that 'it has a whole institutional apparatus that has made it *the* celebrated food' (DuPuis 2002: 217, emphasis in original). This institutional apparatus is both present in institutional form but also through practices and 'hegemonic communities', which makes the implementation of alternatives difficult.

The political economies of milk production are one part of this institutional apparatus. Milk production takes place largely in smallholder farms, where margins are already slim and the risks of taking on alternatives may be seen as high unless there are clear and secure alternative markets. Many farms are heavily invested in capital assets (cows, milking machines, storage, etc.) which creates inertia in the system, and diverse patterns of farm ownership and tenancy across Europe mean that there is significant variation in both the nature and capacities of these agents of change at the farm level. Furthermore, encouraged by agricultural policies and subsidy frameworks (Choplin 2019), currently the supply of milk exceeds demand. Changing the subsidy system could encourage farmers to adopt new technologies and reduce GHG reductions in agriculture. There are also critical gains to be made by working with the largest dairy firms. A report by the US-based Institute for Agriculture and Trade Policy found in 2020 that the world's largest 13 dairy firms were responsible for GHG emissions equivalent to the United Kingdom and rising (Sharma 2020). This suggests that any prospects for decarbonising the industry will need to work with these large firms in order to generate the momentum required to decarbonise this part of the economy.

At the same time, milk's place in the Western cultural politics also conveys significant inertia. In both Western Europe and North America, dairy consumption has been directly linked to the development of the welfare state after World War 2, such that dairy consumption has become an established part of daily routines and national cultures (DuPuis 2002; Jönsson 2005). For example, school milk programmes have been developed to integrate milk into children's diets across Europe such as through the provision of subsidies for the provision of milk with school lunches, which is now a EU policy. Not only are school milk programmes a means to address short-term concerns around access to nutrition as well as the oversupply of milk (Valenze 2011), but also a means to 'normalise' the drinking of milk in order to ensure a steady supply of willing customers into the future. These programmes continue to this day, suggesting that the sites through which decarbonisation will need to take place are highly diverse.

Proponents of dairy milk have also sought to use the institutional apparatus of food standards to protect their product from incomers and ensure the resilience of existing scientific and cultural understandings of milk (Atkins 2010). Accompanying the growth of plant-based alternatives to meat and dairy products, resistance by meat and dairy producers has grown, and has primarily targeted 'standards of identity'. These are standards that specify what products can be called. Dairy producers in the United States, Europe, and Australia are trying to ensure that plant-based alternatives are not allowed to use the word 'milk' in their name but are only allowed to refer to themselves as a 'drink' or 'beverage', for example. From a legal perspective, this therefore means that plant-based drinks are neither milk nor akin to milk (Jönsson et al. 2019).

While the politics of milk's decarbonisation have perhaps been less apparent than those connected to meat, it is clear that milk's future is now hotly contested. As we set out at the start of the section, the milk economy of Europe is unusual amongst emissions-intensive sectors in being highly regionally specific – despite the growth of international markets, most milk produced in Europe is still consumed here. Yet decarbonising milk remains a sticky issue – the EU has long sought to protect the rural economy from economic hardship and the interweaving of political, economic, and cultural factors has served to secure milk a stronghold in the heart of European diets. At the same time, home-grown alternatives represent a real opportunity for new green economies and the transition away from milk-based farming has the potential to also deliver benefits for animal welfare and biodiversity, issues which are also at the forefront of EU concerns. There is a potential for the EU to develop these alternative markets, and there is perhaps a critical window of opportunity to do so as these products are increasingly attracting public interest whilst the dairy industry is seeking to expand to global markets. Reducing milk's imprint globally will require EU dairy industry to reduce its ambitions for growth, whilst also generating the capacity for alternatives. Large dairy companies such as Arla and Danone are increasingly seeking to develop plant-based alternatives, yet in doing so it will be critical that they contribute to a just transition for the dairy farmers who view such alternatives as undermining their livelihoods. Furthermore, while the involvement of incumbents in the switch to plant-based milks is encouraging, there is a risk that this will make plant-based milk, what Goldstein (2018, cited in Jönsson et al. 2019: 85) calls a 'non-disruptive disruption': a technological solution that does not substantially change the underlying causes of the problem. The true disruptive potential of plant-based milk, therefore, remains to be seen. Yet it is clear that without radically rethinking milk and the demand for it in our everyday diets, the possibilities for decarbonisation remain limited.

7 Conclusion

The deadline for decarbonising Europe's economies by 2050 is rapidly approaching. As we suggested at the start of this Element, while much of the focus has been on those parts of society where carbon is highly visible – power generation and mobility, buildings, and aviation – there are an altogether stickier set of problems to be addressed in the carbon-intensive sectors of the economy if net zero is to move from being a dream to a reality. While often hidden from view, steel, paper, plastic, meat, and milk form part of our high-carbon lives on a daily basis. In fact, arguably, they are so normal that so far across the social sciences, we have largely failed to imagine them in a net-zero world, to consider how they could be produced differently, how societies might function with alternatives in place, or how we could come to live without them. As we have sought to demonstrate in the proceeding sections, this is now an urgent task.

Our analysis suggests that there is no settled pathway through which decarbonisation can or will take place. While multiple scenarios and roadmaps exist, we find that there are conflicting visions about what it means to move to net zero across these economies and that multiple, more or less compatible, options are in play. As such, we are not so much confronted with a clear choice between different pathways to decarbonisation – as if standing at the ultimate climate crossroads – but rather faced with the challenge of navigating a way forward when it is clear that diverse approaches are needed, while equally fundamental incompatibilities may serve to undermine progress. For example, approaches that seek to reduce demand may be compromised by those that require continued growth in demand to justify the upfront costs of technological innovations to remove carbon from industrial processes. On the other hand, the development of alternative products, for example, in terms of meat or milk, seems to play a role in more than one pathway to decarbonisation. As a result, some choices for decarbonisation may unlock new possibilities while others that appear straightforward can (unintentionally) prevent alternative options from being on the table, serve to limit or constrain our imagination, and perhaps even lock-in a lower-carbon future but one which is far away from the goals we need to attain (see also, Bernstein and Hoffmann 2019).

Decarbonisation Pathways

Each of the sectors we have examined – steel, plastic, paper, meat, and milk – vary considerably both in terms of where the carbon is to be found, the material and technological possibilities for decarbonisation, the political economies and agents of change through which contested futures are both imagined and realised, and the ways in which their decarbonisation is geographically configured. Yet despite these differences, we find that in each sector, five different imagined futures are being articulated – to greater or lesser extent – as a means through which decarbonisation can be enacted (Table 1). These imagined futures can be articulated by certain actors – for example, incumbent actors may advocate more reformist rather than radical positions – but equally this is not settled, as both dominant actors and new arrivals identify potential opportunities on the road ahead. At the same time, unlikely coalitions of actors are being formed around each vision, bringing together in different combinations incumbent industries, workers, environmental groups, consumers, and so on. As a result, there are few certainties in terms of diagnosing which kinds of imagined worlds will be more or less dominant, as each encounter particular challenges when they come to be translated into the specific contexts of these carbon-intensive sectors of the economy.

First, it is clear that across these sectors the notion of ***energy efficiency*** remains in pole position as the means through which they are intending to realise decarbonisation. Yet, unlike in other sectors where decarbonisation pathways are increasingly well-trodden – housing, vehicles, electrical appliances, manufacturing processes – efficiency measures may appear to have only limited potential. This is in part because in some sectors, and here meat and milk stand out, the bulk of carbon is not to be found in the processes through which products are made but instead in the very material basis – animals and agricultural land – from which they are made. It is also a reflection of gains which have already been made in some industries (e.g. paper) and that the opportunities for making such investments are sporadic, being undertaken primarily at the end-of-life of particular equipment or where other external pressures force the introduction of new technologies. In the absence of such opportunities, a focus has then turned to how such sectors can be made ***carbon efficient*** increasing the use of renewable electricity and biomass, developing new land management practices that reduce the impact on climate change, and by technologies that seek to capture carbon emissions or schemes that offer carbon-offsetting for

Table 1 Prospective decarbonisation pathways for steel, plastic, paper, meat and milk

Decarbonisation is …	Steel	Plastic	Paper	Meat	Milk
Producing things better – reducing the carbon content of production	Reduce fossil-energy energy use in production. Increase the efficiency of the steel making process e.g., improving heat integration in iron and steel mills. Capture the carbon (CCS, CCU).	Reduce fossil-energy energy use in production. Increase the efficiency of the plastic making process, e.g., more efficient equipment for separation and compression. Supply heat with renewable electricity instead of gas in steam crackers.	Reduce fossil-energy energy use in production using e.g., biofuels, including renewable alternatives to operate the lime kiln. Increase the efficiency of the paper making process e.g., use of waste residues as fuel, new paper drying technologies.	Reduce fossil-fuel energy use in the processing and transport of meat. Agro-forestry and carbon offsetting schemes to compensate for carbon contribution.	Reduce fossil-fuel energy use in the processing and transport of milk. Agro-forestry and carbon offsetting schemes to compensate for carbon contribution e.g., Arla carbon offsetting programs.

Producing things differently – using different materials to reduce the carbon input	Green electricity, bio-coke, or green hydrogen-based iron and steel production.	Substitute carbon feedstock (oil) with bio-based feedstock (sugar, maize or agricultural residues) e.g., bio-PET (30% bio-based plastic) or PEF (100% bio-based plastic) plastic bottles.	Grass, straw or similar simple fibres instead of wood for low-quality or single use board. Biorefineries: produce more diverse outputs than just paper.	Smart agriculture e.g., changes the gut microbiome of cows, dietary substitutes. Reduce the energy intensity of material inputs, e.g., free range and organic farming. Produce alternative meat through laboratory process.	Smart agriculture, e.g., change the gut microbiome of cows, dietary substitutes. Reduce the energy intensity of material inputs, e.g., free range and organic farming. Produce alternative milk or whey through laboratory process, to be used by e.g., ice-cream makers and dairy companies.

Table 1 (cont.)

Decarbonisation is . . .	Steel	Plastic	Paper	Meat	Milk
Doing more with less carbon – reusing and recycling materials	Recycling scrap steel. Reusing steel reclaimed from buildings.	Business-to-business reuse strategies for packaging. Requirements on recyclability for different types of products.	More recycling, higher rates. Connecting recycling loops for different fibres and applications, e.g., paper, board, and textiles.	Avoid wasting food. Reconnect producers with consumers through ethics of care, e.g., Open Food Network.	Avoid wasting food. Reconnect producers with consumers through ethics of care, e.g., Open Food Network.
Using lower carbon alternatives – substituting high carbon goods and services	Replace some steel with wood in the building sector e.g., 'Plyscrapers'	Paper or other alternatives to single-use plastic (e.g., straws, plates, nappies, hygiene products).	Multi-use products instead of single-use paper: paper plates vs. ceramics.	Plant-based protein e.g., impossible burger, soy-based dietary substitutes.	Plant-based milk.
Consuming less high carbon products and services or learning to live without them	Use office space more efficiently and avoid steel cans.	Avoiding clothing with fossil-fuel based fibres. Restricting plastic to few necessary uses e.g., medical settings. Using zero-waste supermarkets.	Paperless office. Reusable containers (glass or steel).	Meatless Monday. Less but better meat. Vegetarianism. Veganism.	Veganism.

production. Notably, there is significant optimism about the potential to expand renewable electricity and biomass provision such that it can meet the needs of individual industrial sectors, but in any one sector limited consideration is given to how their requirements will be met whilst also enabling decarbonisation of housing and mobility across Europe. There is also significant hope invested in the capacities of carbon capture technologies, despite there yet being any widespread demonstrable use of this technology at scale or its development taking place on a timescale that would be compatible with realising 2050 goals for net zero.

Second, we see pathways that emerge around how things could be produced differently. The focus here is on changing the ***material basis of production*** such that while they retain the same physical and cultural qualities, their carbon input is reduced. For example, SSAB, a major Swedish steel producer, aims to bring fossil-free steel to the market by 2026, through changing the ways in which steel is produced (no longer dependent on metallurgical coal, but on hydrogen or electrolysis powered by renewable electricity). To substitute the material feedstock needed to produce things is a popular pathway to follow. Here we see the bioplastic economy, with bio-based materials being used to create plastic, and the rise of the fibre economy, with wood fibres being used to produce substitutes to, for example, single-use plastic. There are emergent land-use conflicts ahead in terms of competition for what to grow (food vs fibres) and where to grow it both because of the limited resources available and in order to avoid negative impacts on natural habitats that are important for the function of ecosystems and the preservation of biodiversity. While material substitution for fossil-plastic products is increasingly common, changing how meat and milk are made raise a rather different set of issues. Hacking a cow's gut bacteria (to produce less methane through burps and farts) is still mostly at the stage of controlled experiments by animal scientists. New ways of growing meat and milk directly in the lab has received more attention, not least from venture capitalist funds, suggesting that these pathways to decarbonisation will rely on the dynamics of financialisation (Mouat and Prince 2018). Yet despite the emphasis on developing alternatives, we find that the prospects for sustaining their consumption rely on preserving their cultural qualities. Bioplastic Lego should feel and sound the same as plastic Lego, and synthetic meat is fashioned so that its taste and appearance, of a meat-like texture that 'bleeds', preserves our understanding of what meat should be. The plastic industry calls for 'drop-in solutions' – those that can be seamlessly integrated into the current production infrastructure with limited changes required and where the cultural qualities and functions of the products are retained.

A third set of pathways involves putting existing materials back into circulation through reuse and recycling in order to ***do more with less carbon***. For some this pathway rests on the growth of the circular economy. In the paper sector, we see that this is a vision that already has a history, such that the market for recycled paper is firmly established. Yet paper has distinct qualities that allow for its circulation which are much harder to find in plastic where issues of the material composition, geographical spread, and lock-in of certain kinds of material over time mean that recycling and repurposing is still marginal to the mainstream economy. To some extent, imposed requirements on recyclability for different types of products may allow for more circulation, and the economic viability of the pathway will rest on whether recycling loops across a range of different materials and applications can be established. Doing more with less is shaping pathways emerging within the economies of meat and milk, where the wasting of food (from the farm to the dinner table) has been established as a key challenge. While for steel, plastic, and paper ideas of doing more with less have tended to lean towards reducing the material throughput and ensuring its (re) circulation, in food economies we find alternative approaches which seek to more fundamentally change their structure and form by reducing the length of supply chains and also placing an ethics of care at their centre. At the same time, the imperative of reducing food waste is often used as a rationale for the use of more plastic and paper packaging materials to reduce damage and preserve goods over time, showing again the intricate interlinkages between the pathways across these sectors.

Fourth, we find a manifold of innovations in pathways that revolve around the **substitution** of high-carbon goods and services. Here the physical properties of the materials used are changed in order to produce lower-carbon alternatives that still retain some of the qualities that our familiar products hold. Emerging alternatives have the same look and feel as things that we are familiar with, but where their new carbon credentials are used as a persuasive selling point – whether it be for skyscrapers made of wood, paper bottles, or oat-based milk. In the food economy, the growth of alternatives to meat and milk has been rapid over recent years, such that is arguably becoming established as its own food sector as everyday food materials (oats, lentils, soy protein, peas) are repurposed to (re)produce meatiness and milky-ness. As with those alternative products which rely on different feedstock or processes to produce the-same-but-lower-carbon products, what is notable about these alternatives which rely on wholly different materials is that they also need to reproduce the standards and qualities of the original products – milk should be white, alternative meats should be able to reproduce family dinners (from Shepherd's Pie in the United Kingdom to Swedish meatballs), bamboo plates should be as light, pliable, and disposable as their plastic ascendants, and so on. Where new interventions for decarbonisation have been most successful, it is where they reproduce and perform our current ways of living. Yet at the same time, we see strong attempts to marginalise or side-line these alternatives from incumbent interests – for example, with those who produce 'real' milk stressing its nutritional qualities and health benefits, or with alternative building materials being regulated by the same standards that are applied to steel. It appears that innovations in the carbon-intensive sectors of the economy are still required to 'fit and conform' to existing socio-technical systems (Smith and Raven 2012), suggesting that their potential for realising truly transformational change may be limited.

Finally, we also find some evidence that there are pathways emerging around notions of **living (well) with less.** In terms of the cases that we have explored in this Element, it is primarily in the food and plastic economies that we see the emergence of these visions which rest on reducing demand, at least partly drawing on the notion of sufficiency. These are arguably the most consumer-facing sectors, and where consumer behaviour can most readily start to reshape markets. But demanding less is quite demanding. Seen from the perspectives of today, these are either seen as banal ('drop in the ocean' from reducing single-use plastics), unaffordable (designed for high-end consumers), or too overtly radically political (e.g. veganism or plastic-free shopping). As a result, and because the policy imagination of sustainability transitions remains dominated by visions of technological innovation and economic efficiencies, such inter-ventions are readily dismissed by policymakers and businesses. Yet this is a significant missed opportunity, for what these pathways indicate is that any effort to make a shift to a decarbonised world will require cultural and political change alongside shifts which are instigated by new technologies or economic incentives. Rather than reading such interventions as ephemeral to the main business of decarbonisation, we suggest we need to see them as containing important grains of insight that provide grist to the mill of decarbonisation.

Future Present

As the American writer William Gibson once said, 'the future is already here – it's just not very evenly distributed'. Despite the narratives of the urgency of the problem and heroic assumptions about what it will be possible for society to do to reach net zero, for the most part the future of decarbonisation is already here. Following Gibson, and looking across the sections in this Element, we suggest that a 'climate-neutral Europe' is (soon) already here – the challenge is that it is currently situated in specific sites and arenas rather than being more evenly distributed. Rather than imagining pathways for decarbonisation as a journey from where we are now to some unknown future, in *Decarbonising Economies*, we have approached the question of what it will mean to arrive at net zero from a different perspective – to understand actually existing decarbonisation and what this tells us about the challenges we will need to navigate.

Across the sections in this Element we see how different visions of, on the one hand, technological options, and, on the other hand, changes in behaviours and cultures, shape the realm of the possible. Here we need to remind ourselves of the power at work in our visions, expectations, or even assumptions, of the future. To what extent visions of the technical or the social are understood as implementable, costly, marginal or radical is a matter of perspective and position. Imagination is a social practice; it is shared by members of a community and we can follow how it becomes embedded into cultures, institutions, and materialities. When technological futures gain traction into wider circuits of capital and authority, they start to project futures as they ought to be, having the power to move minds and actions at a distance (Jasanoff 2015: 323). The role we assign to CCS-technology or to plastics recycling in the future shape the perceived importance of taking other possible measures in the present.

Critically, we have found that there are multiple pathways emerging for decarbonising economies and that it is likely that all will have a role to play in shifting the economy to net zero, even while they will conflict with one another. Decarbonisation is not a smooth process but a fragmented and con-tested set of interventions that have more or less scope and capacity to reach their desired destination. In part, this is a matter of technical prowess. Radical technological and material changes are needed to how we produce some of our most basic, used, and loved materials. Yet it is also clear that there are insuffi-cient resources – of land, power, feedstock, and finance – for all of the technical dreams to come true. And that some pathways imply that the burdens and benefits of decarbonisation will be highly uneven, such that there is a vital need to consider the justice implications of any such interventions. Remaking the decarbonised world in the image of the high-carbon economies which we currently inhabit appears to guide pathways which not only seek to be more carbon efficient, but also those which seek to develop material alternatives or substitutes that can readily slot into our existing senses of what counts as a good life. There is much more limited evidence that in the ambition to decarbonise our economies we are engaging in questions about what it is we need to sustain, for whom, and on what basis – of why we need to use oil to produce grass or eat meat to be masculine.

Without engaging in such a dialogue, it is unlikely that the dreams of a climate-neutral Europe by 2050 will come to fruition. To be sure, great strides are being taken within the policy arena across Europe to realise this ambition – not least the decision in 2020 by the European Parliament to pursue a reduction of 60 per cent carbon by 2030 and the extensive support offered to such ambition by the Green Deal programme. Yet ensuring that the kinds of decarbonisation we already have to hand become more evenly spread, that the low-carbon futures that have come to be familiar through the pages of this Element circulate and come to settle across Europe will take a sustained effort. This will require more from both those promoting these innovations and those incumbent actors who have committed to change. With strong policy support, available finance, a willing public, and businesses who see such shifts as being in their long-term interest, if such efforts cannot be made in Europe it is unlikely that they can succeed elsewhere. The question is perhaps not one of ambition – for there seems to be plenty of that – but of courage. Too often action for decarbonisation is delayed not as a result of overt opposition but as a result of the optimism placed in new technologies or policies that appear to be just around the corner and whose arrival will herald the real momentum for change. In this case, the perfect climate solution appears to be the enemy of the good – we have already been waiting too long for this perfect storm to bring forth the kind of action on climate change the world needs. Replacing this optimistic outlook with a courageous one means imagining that the solutions we already have, here to hand, can be a good enough place to start – that we do not need to wait for new technologies or political commitments, that we can start now. It also takes courage to recognise that as we navigate pathways to decarbonised futures we will need to allow for diverse approaches, to live with imperfect outcomes and be ready to encounter failure as much as we succeed.

References

Aan den Toorn, S. I., Tziva, M., van den Broek, M. A., Negro, S. O., Hekkert, M. P., and Worrell, E., 2018. Climate innovations in meat and dairy. Project Deliverable 2.5, H2020 REINVENT Project Nr 730053. https://www.reinvent-project.eu/s/updated-D25-Climate-innovations-in-meat-and-dairy.pdf

Aan den Toorn, S. I., Worrell, E., and van den Broek, M. A., 2021. How much can combinations of measures reduce methane and nitrous oxide emissions from European livestock husbandry and feed cultivation? *Journal of Cleaner Production*, 304, 127138.

Adler, D. and Wargan, P., 2019. Ursula von der Leyen's Green Deal is doomed. *Politico*. www.politico.eu/article/ursula-von-der-leyens-green-deal-is-doomed-climate-change-european-commission/

Aggestam, F., Konczal, A., Sotirov, M., Wallin, I., Paillet, Y., Spinelli, R., Lindner, M., Derks, J., Hanewinkel, M., and Winkel, G., 2020. Can nature conservation and wood production be reconciled in managed forests? A review of driving factors for integrated forest management in Europe. *Journal of Environmental Management*, 268, 110670.

AkzoNobel, 2017. AkzoNobel to be carbon neutral and use 100% renewable energy by 2050. www.akzonobel.com/en/for-media/media-releases-and-features/akzonobel-be-carbon-neutral-and-use-100-renewable-energy-2050

Alén, R., 2018. Manufacturing cellulosic fibres for making paper: A historical perspective. In Särkkä, T., Gutiérrez-Poch, M., and Kuhlberg, M. (eds.) *Technological Transformation in the Global Pulp and Paper Industry*. Comparative Perspectives. Cham: Springer, pp. 1800–2018.

Allwood, J. M., Cullen, J. M., and Milford, R. L., 2010. Options for achieving a 50% cut in industrial carbon emissions by 2050. *Environmental Science & Technology*, 44(6), 1888–94. http://doi.org/10.1021/es902909k

AP News, 2018. Cultured meat (poultry, pork, beef, duck) market – Global forecast to 2027 – ResearchAndMarkets.com. www.apnews.com/e46c4b5af8854db7bfa158005e27fae1

ArcelorMittal, 2020. Climate action in Europe – Our carbon emissions reduction roadmap: 30% by 2030 and carbon neutral by 2050. https://corporate-media.arcelormittal.com/media/yw1gnzfo/climate-action-in-europe.pdf

Arla, 2019a. Arla foods aims for carbon net zero dairy. www.arla.com/company/news-and-press/2019/pressrelease/arla-foods-aims-for-carbon-net-zero-dairy-2845602/

Arla, 2019b. Farming for the future – Towards sustainable dairy farming. www .arla.com/food-for-thought/sustainability/farming-for-the-future-towards-sustainable-dairy-farming/

Arla, 2019c. Green ambition 2050. www.arla.com/493b98/globalassets/arla-global/sustainability/climate-ambition/arla_201902_08.pdf

Atkins, P., 2010. *Liquid Materialities: A History of Milk, Science and the Law.* London: Routledge.

Audsley, E., Brander, M., Chatterton, J., Murphy-Bo kern, D. , Webster, C., and Williams, A., 2009. How low can we go? An assessment of greenhouse gas emissions from the UK food system and the scope to reduce them by 2050. World Wide Fund for Nature (WWF), Godalming. https://assets.wwf.org.uk/ downloads/how_low_report_1.pdf

Bauer, F., Coenen, L., Hansen, T., McCormick, K., and Voytenko Palgan, Y., 2017. Technological innovation systems for biorefineries: A review of the literature. *Biofuels, Bioproducts and Biorefining*, 11(3), 534–48. http://doi .org/10.1002/bbb.1767

Befort, N., 2020. Going beyond definitions to understand tensions within the bioeconomy: The contribution of sociotechnical regimes to contested fields. *Technological Forecasting and Social Change*, 153, 119923.

Bellevrat, E. and Menanteau, P., 2009. Introducing carbon constraint in the steel sector: ULCOS scenarios and economic modelling. *Revue de Métallurgie*, 106 (9), 318–324. Selected papers from 4th ULCOS SEMINAR (Part 1) http://doi.org/10.1051/metal/2009059

Bergquist, A.-K. and Söderholm, K., 2018. The greening of the pulp and paper industry: Sweden in comparative perspective. In Särkkä, T., Gutiérrez-Poch, M., and Kuhlberg, M. (eds.) *Technological Transformation in the Global Pulp and Paper Industry.* Comparative Perspectives. Cham: Springer, pp. 1800–2018.

Bernstein, S. and Hoffmann, M., 2018. The politics of decarbonization and the catalytic impact of subnational climate experiments. *Policy Sciences*, 51(2), 189–211. http://doi.org/10.1007/s11077-018-9314-8

Bernstein, S. and Hoffmann, M., 2019. Climate politics, metaphors and the fractal carbon trap. *Nature Climate Change*, 9, 919–25.

Best, J. and Paterson, M., 2009. *Cultural Political Economy.* London: Routledge.

Borrelle, S. B., Rochman, C. M., Liboiron, M., Bond, A. L., Lusher, A., Bradshaw, H., and Provencher, J. F., 2017. Opinion: Why we need an international agreement on marine plastic pollution. *Proceedings of the National Academy of Sciences*, 114(38), 9994–7. http://doi.org/10.1073/ pnas.1714450114

Brandner, R., Flatscher, G., Ringhofer, A., Schickhofer, G., and Thiel, A., 2016. Cross laminated timber (CLT): overview and development. *European Journal of Wood Products*, 74, 331–51. http://doi.org/10.1016/j .engstruct.2018.05.060

Broeren, M. L. M., Saygin, D., and Patel, M. K., 2014. Forecasting global developments in the basic chemical industry for environmental policy analysis. *Energy Policy*, 64, 273–87. http://doi.org/10.1016/j.enpol.2013.09.025

Brun, L., 2016. Overcapacity in steel: China's role in a global problem. Center on Globalization, Governance & Competitiveness, Duke University, Durham, USA. http://doi.org/10.13140/RG.2.2.11923.48161

Brunnhofer, M., Gabriella, N., Schöggl, J.-P., Stern, T., and Posch, A., 2020. The biorefinery transition in the European pulp and paper industry – A three-phase Delphi study including a SWOT-AHP analysis. *Forest Policy and Economics*, 110, 101882. http://doi.org/10.1016/j.forpol.2019.02.006

C40, 2019. In focus: Building and infrastructure consumption emissions. The C40 Cities Climate Leadership Group, London and University of Leeds. https://c40-production-images.s3.amazonaws.com/other_uploads/images/ 2390_BIC_Report_FINAL.original.pdf?1570401598

Carus, M. and Raschka, A., 2018. Nova position paper chemistry 2050: Renewable carbon is key to a sustainable and future-oriented chemical industry. nova-Institute, Hürth. : https://www.biobased.us/pdf/18-08-03-nova-Paper10-Renewable-Carbon-Copy.pdf

Catts, O. and Zurr, I., 2004. Disembodied meat. *Cabinet Magazine*, 16. www .cabinetmagazine.org/issues/16/catts_zurr.php

CEFIC, 2019. Molecule managers: A journey into the future of Europe with the European chemical industry. The European Chemical Industry Council (CEFIC), Brussels. https://cefic.org/app/uploads/2019/06/Cefic_Mid-Century-Vision-Molecule-Managers-Brochure.pdf

CEFIC and Ecofys, 2013. European chemistry for growth – Unlocking a competitive, low-carbon and energy efficient future. The European Chemical Industry Council (CEFIC), Brussels. https://cefic.org/app/ uploads/2019/01/Energy-Roadmap-The-Report-European-chemistry-for-growth_BROCHURE-Energy.pdf

CEPI, n.d. CEPI website. www.cepi.org/

CEPI, 2011. The forest fibre industry 2050 roadmap to a low-carbon bio-economy. Confederation of European Paper Industries (CEPI), Brussels. https://www.cepi.org/wp-content/uploads/2020/08/2050_roadmap_final.pdf

CEPI, 2020. Key statistics 2019 – European pulp and paper industry. Confederation of European Paper Industries (CEPI), Brussels. https://www .cepi.org/wp-content/uploads/2020/07/Final-Key-Statistics-2019.pdf

Chertkovskaya, E., Holmberg, K., Petersén, M., Stripple, J., and Ullström, S., 2020. Making visible, rendering obscure: Reading the plastic crisis through contemporary artistic visual representations. *Global Sustainability*, 3, e14.

Choplin, G., 2019. Let's not export our problems. European Milk Board, Brussels. www.europeanmilkboard.org/fileadmin/Subsite/Afrika/ Brochure_campagnelait_court_EN.pdf

CIEL, 2017. Fueling plastics: Fossils, plastics, and petrochemical feedstocks. Center for International Environmental Law (CIEL), Washington, DC. https://www.ciel.org/wp-content/uploads/2017/09/Fueling-Plastics-Fossils-Plastics-Petrochemical-Feedstocks.pdf

Clark, M. and Tilman, D., 2017. Comparative analysis of environmental impacts of agricultural production systems, agricultural input efficiency, and food choice. *Environmental Research Letters*, 12, 064016.

Crang, M., Hughes, A., Gregson, N., Norris, L., and Ahamed, F. U., 2013. Rethinking governance and value in commodity chains through global recycling networks. *Transactions of the Institute of British Geographers*, 38(1), 12–24.

Danone, 2019. Towards carbon neutrality. www.danone.com/impact/planet/ towards-carbon-neutrality.html

de Besi, M. and McCormick, K., 2015. Towards a bioeconomy in Europe: National, regional and industrial strategies. *Sustainability*, 7(8), 10461–78. http://doi.org/10.3390/su70810461

de Blasio, B., 2019. Mayor de Blasio announces New York City's green new deal. www1.nyc.gov/office-of-the-mayor/news/211-19/transcript-mayor-de-blasio-new-york-city-s-green-new-deal

DECHEMA, 2017. Technology study – Low carbon energy and feedstock for the European chemical industry. https://cefic.org/app/uploads/2019/01/Low-carbon-energy-and-feedstock-for-the-chemical-industry-DECHEMA_Report-energy_climate.pdf

deFrance, S. D., 2009. Zooarchaeology in complex societies: Political economy, status, and ideology. *Journal of Archaeological Research*, 17(2), 105–68.

DG ENV Official, 2018. Governmental body of the European Commission. DG ENV – The Directorate-General for Environment (Interview conducted on the 26 November 2018).

DuPuis, E. M., 2002. *Nature's Perfect Food: How Milk Became America's Drink*. New York: New York University Press.

ECIU, 2020. Net zero tracker. Energy & Climate Intelligence Unit (ECIU), London. http://eciu.net/netzerotracker/map

Ellen MacArthur Foundation, n.d. Our vision for a circular economy for plastics. https://ellenmacarthurfoundation.org/plastics-vision

Ellen MacArthur Foundation, 2016. The new plastics economy: Rethinking the future of plastics. World Economic Forum and Ellen MacArthur Foundation, Cowes. https://emf.thirdlight.com/link/faarmdpz93ds-5vmvdf/@/preview/1?o

Ellen MacArthur Foundation, 2017. A new textiles economy: Redesigning fashion's future. Ellen MacArthur Foundation, Cowes. https://emf.third light.com/link/2axvc7eob8zx-za4ule/@/preview/1?o

Ellen MacArthur Foundation, 2019. Reuse: Rethinking Packaging. Ellen MacArthur Foundation, Cowes. https://emf.thirdlight.com/link/rzv910prtxn-tfiulo/@/#id=1

Elzen, B., Geels, F. W., Hofman, P. S., and Green, K., 2004. Socio-technical scenarios as a tool for transition policy: An example from the traffic and transport domain. In Elzen, B., Geels, F. W., and Green, K. (eds.) *System Innovation and the Transition to Sustainability: Theory, Evidence and Policy.* Cheltenham/ Northampton: Edward Elgar, pp. 251–81.

Energy and Climate Bill No. 1908, 2019. www.assemblee-nationale.fr/dyn/15/textes/l15b1908_projet-loi

Environmental Audit Committee, 2018. Disposable packaging: Coffee cups. House of Commons, 2nd Report of Session 2017–19, London.

EUROFER, 2019. Low carbon roadmap – Pathways to a CO_2-neutral European steel industry. The European Steel Industry Association, Brussels. www.eurofer.eu/assets/Uploads/EUROFER-Low-Carbon-Roadmap-Pathways-to-a-CO2-neutral-European-Steel-Industry.pdf

European Commission, 2015. EU ETS handbook. European Commission, Brussels.

European Commission, 2017. Roadmap: Strategy on plastics in a circular economy. https://ec.europa.eu/smart-regulation/roadmaps/docs/plan_2016_39_plastic_strategy_en.pdf

European Commission, 2018a. A clean planet for all – A European strategic long-term vision for a prosperous, modern, competitive and climate neutral economy. COM(2018) 773 final, Brussels. https://eur-lex.europa.eu/legal-content/EN/TXT/PDF/?uri=CELEX:52018DC0773

European Commission, 2018b. A European strategy for plastics in a circular economy. COM(2018) 28 final Brussels. https://eur-lex.europa.eu/legal-content/EN/TXT/?uri=COM:2018:28:FIN

European Commission, 2018c. Evaluation study of the impact of the CAP on climate change and greenhouse gas emissions. Directorate-General for Agriculture and Rural Development, Brussels. https://op.europa.eu/en/publication-detail/-/publication/29eee93e-9ed0-11e9-9d01-01aa75ed71a1

European Commission, 2019a. EU green public procurement criteria for food, catering services and vending machines. Commission Staff Working

Document, SWD(2019) 366 final, Brussels. https://ec.europa.eu/environment/ gpp/pdf/190927_EU_GPP_criteria_for_food_and_catering_services_SWD_ (2019)_366_final.pdf

European Commission, 2019b. A European green deal. https://ec.europa.eu/ info/strategy/priorities-2019-2024/european-green-deal_en

European Commission, 2020. A new industrial strategy for Europe. COM (2020) 102 final, Brussels. https://eur-lex.europa.eu/legal-content/EN/TXT/ PDF/?uri=CELEX:52020DC0102&from=EN

Eurostat, 2018. Milk and milk product statistics. https://ec.europa.eu/eurostat/ statistics-explained/index.php/Milk_and_milk_product_statistics

FAO, 2011. Global food losses and food waste – Extent, causes and prevention. Food and Agriculture Organization of the United Nations (FAO), Rome. www.fao.org/3/a-i2697e.pdf

FAO, 2019a. Yearbook of forest products 2017. Food and Agriculture Organization of the United Nations (FAO), Rome. https://www.fao.org/3/ ca5703m/CA5703M.pdf

FAO, 2019b. Dairy animals. Food and Agriculture Organization of the United Nations (FAO), Rome. www.fao.org/dairy-production-products/production/ dairy-animals/cattle/en/

FAO, 2019c. Dairy market review. Food and Agriculture Organization of the United Nations (FAO), Rome. www.fao.org/3/ca3879en/ca3879en.pdf

FAO and GDP, 2018. Climate change and the global dairy cattle sector. Food and Agriculture Organization of the United Nations (FAO) and Global Dairy Platform Inc (GDP), Rome. https://dairysustainabilityframework.org/wp-con tent/uploads/2019/01/Climate-Change-and-the-Global-Dairy-Cattle-Sector.pdf

Fernandez-Pales, A. and Levi, P., 2018. The future of petrochemicals: Towards more sustainable plastics and fertilisers. International Energy Agency (IEA), Paris. https://iea.blob.core.windows.net/assets/bee4ef3a-8876-4566-98cf- 7a130c013805/The_Future_of_Petrochemicals.pdf

Fischer, W., Hake, J.-F., Kuckshinrichs, W., Schröder, T., and Venghaus, S., 2016. German energy policy and the way to sustainability: Five controversial issues in the debate on the 'Energiewende'. *Energy*, 115, 1580–91.

Flanders Agency of Innovation and Entrepreneurship, 2019. Compensatie indirecte emissiekosten. www.vlaio.be/nl/subsidies-financiering/subsidieda tabank/compensatie-indirecte-emissiekosten

Froggatt, A. and Wellesley, L., 2019. Meat analogues: Considerations for the EU. Chatham House, The Royal Institute of International Affairs, London. https://www.chathamhouse.org/sites/default/files/2020-12/2019-02-18- meat-analogues.pdf

Geels, F. W., 2019. Socio-technical transitions to sustainability: A review of criticisms and elaborations of the multi-level perspective. *Current Opinion in Environmental Sustainability*, 39, 187–201. http://doi.org/10.1016/j.cosust.2019.06.009

Gerber, P. J., Steinfeld, H., Henderson, B., Mottet, A., Opio, C., Dijkman, J., Falucci, A., and Tempio, G., 2013. Tackling climate change through livestock: A global assessment of emissions and mitigation opportunities. Food and Agriculture Organization of the United Nations (FAO), Rome. www.fao.org/3/i3437e/i3437e00.htm

Geyer, R., Jambeck, J. R., and Law, K. L., 2017. Production, use, and fate of all plastics ever made. *Science Advances*, 3(7), p.e1700782.

Giesekam, J. and Pomponi, F., 2017. Embodied carbon dioxide assessment in buildings: Guidance and gaps. *ICE – Engineering Sustainability*, 171(7), 334–41. http://doi.org/10.1680/jensu.17.00032

Global Carbon Atlas, 2020. CO_2 emissions. www.globalcarbonatlas.org/en/CO2-emissions

Haarstad, H. and Wanvik, T. I., 2016. Carbonscapes and beyond. *Progress in Human Geography*, 41(4), 432–50. http://doi.org/10.1177/0309132516648007

Hagberg, J., 2016. Agencing practices: A historical exploration of shopping bags. *Consumption Markets and Culture*, 19(1), 111–32.

Hamilton, L. A. and Feit, S., 2019. Plastic and climate: The hidden costs of a plastic planet. Center for International Environmental Law (CIEL), Washington, DC. https://www.ciel.org/wp-content/uploads/2019/05/Plastic-and-Climate-FINAL-2019.pdf

Hancox, D., 2018. The unstoppable rise of veganism: How a fringe movement went mainstream. *The Guardian*. www.theguardian.com/lifeandstyle/2018/apr/01/vegans-are-coming-millennials-health-climate-change-animal-welfare

Hawkins, G., 2018. The skin of commerce: Governing through plastic food packaging. *Journal of Cultural Economy*, 11(5), 386–403.

Heaps, C., Erickson, P., Kartha, S., and Kemp-Benedict, E., 2009. Europe's share of the climate challenge – Domestic actions and international obligations to protect the planet. Stockholm Environment Institute (SEI), Stockholm. www.sei.org/publications/europes-share-climate-challenge/

Hedenus, F., Wirsenius, S., and Johansson, D. J. A., 2014. The importance of reduced meat and dairy consumption for meeting stringent climate change targets. *Climatic Change*, 124, 79–91. https://link.springer.com/article/10.1007percent2Fs10584-014-1104-5

HeidelbergCement, 2019. HeidelbergCement first cement company to receive approval for science-based CO_2 reduction targets. www.heidelbergcement.com/en/pr-13-05-2019

Heinrich-Böll-Stiftung, Rosa Luxemburg Foundation, and Friends of the Earth, 2017. Agrifood atlas: Facts and figures about the corporations that control what we eat. Heinrich-Böll-Stiftung, Berlin; Rosa Luxemburg Foundation, Berlin; Friends of the Earth, Brussels. http://doi.org/10.13140/RG.2.2.32895.51364

Hoffmann, M. and Bernstein, S., 2020. Why action on climate change gets stuck and what to do about it. *The Conversation.* https://theconversation.com/why-action-on-climate-change-gets-stuck-and-what-to-do-about-it-128287

Holmes, M., 2019. The natural alternative. *Compounding World* (3), 29–38.

Hunter, T., 2018. Redefining energy security: The new prize in a time of arctic petroleum resources and technological development. In Raszewski, S. (ed.) *The International Political Economy of Oil and Gas.* Cham: Springer, pp. 9–21.

Huppmann, D., Kriegler, E., Krey, V., Riahi, K., Rogelj, J., Rose, S. K., Weyant, J., Bauer, N., Bertram, C., Bosetti, V., Calvin, K., Doelman, J., Drouet, L., Emmerling, J., Frank, S., Fujimori, S., Gernaat, D., Grubler, A., Guivarch, C., Haigh, M., Holz, C., Iyer, G., Kato, E., Keramidas, K., Kitous, A., Leblanc, F., Liu, J.-Y., Löffler, K., Luderer, G., Marcucci, A., McCollum, D., Mima, S., Popp, A., Sands, R. D., Sano, F., Strefler, J., Tsutsui, J., Van Vuuren, D., Vrontisi, Z., Wise, M., and Zhang, R., 2018. IAMC 1.5°C scenario explorer and data hosted by IIASA. Integrated Assessment Modeling Consortium & International Institute for Applied Systems Analysis. doi: 10.5281/zenodo.3363345

IEA, 2009. Energy technology transitions for industry. Organisation for Economic Co-operation and Development, Paris; International Energy Agency (IEA), Paris. https://doi.org/10.1787/9789264068612-en

IEA, 2016. Energy technology perspectives – Towards sustainable urban energy systems. International Energy Agency (IEA), Paris. www.iea.org/reports/energy-technology-perspectives-2016

IEA, 2017. Energy technology perspectives – Catalysing energy technology transformations. International Energy Agency (IEA), Paris. www.iea.org/reports/energy-technology-perspectives-2017

IEA, 2018. World energy outlook 2018. International Energy Agency (IEA), Paris. www.iea.org/reports/world-energy-outlook-2018

IEA, 2020a. Iron and steel technology roadmap – Towards more sustainable steelmaking. International Energy Agency (IEA), Paris. www.iea.org/reports/iron-and-steel-technology-roadmap

IEA, 2020b. Pulp and paper. International Energy Agency (IEA), Paris. www.iea.org/reports/pulp-and-paper

IISD, 2018. Low-carbon innovation for sustainable infrastructure – The role of public procurement. International Institute for Sustainable Development

(IISD), Winnipeg. https://i2-4c.eu/wp-content/uploads/2018/03/Low-Carbon-Innovation-for-Sustainable-Infrastructure-The-role-of-public-pro curement_v2.2_web.pdf

IPCC, 2019. Special report on climate change and land. Summary for policy makers. Intergovernmental Panel on Climate Change (IPCC), Geneva. www.ipcc.ch/site/assets/uploads/2019/08/Edited-SPM_Approved_Microsite_FINAL.pdf

Jallinoja, P., Vinnari, M., and Niva, M., 2018. Veganism and plant-based eating: Analysis of interplay between discursive strategies and lifestyle political consumerism. In Boström, M., Micheletti, M., and Oosterveer, P. (eds.) *The Oxford Handbook of Political Consumerism*. New York: Oxford University Press, pp. 157–80.

Jasanoff, S. , 2015. Imagined and invented worlds. In Jasanoff, S. and Kim, S. H. (eds.) *Dreamscapes of Modernity: Sociotechnical Imaginaries and the Fabrication of Power*. Chicago: University of Chicago Press, pp. 321–40.

Jernkontoret, 2018. Klimatfärdplan (climate roadmap). Swedish Steel Industry Association, Stockholm. https://www.jernkontoret.se/globalassets/publi cerat/stal-stalind/klimatfardplan2018-1-web.pdf

Johnson, B., 2016. *Zero Waste Home: The Ultimate Guide to Simplifying Your Life*. London: Penguin Books.

Joshi, V. K. and Kumar, S., 2015. Meat analogues: Plant based alternatives to meat products. A review. *International Journal of Food and Fermentation Technology*, 5(2), 107–19.

Judge, M. and Wilson, M. S., 2015. Vegetarian Utopias: Visions of dietary patterns in future societies and support for social change. *Futures*, 71, 57–69.

Jönsson, E., Linné, T., and McCrow-Young, A., 2019. Many meats and many milks? The ontological politics of a proposed post-animal revolution. *Science as Culture*, 28(1), 70–97.

Jönsson, H., 2005. *Mjölk – en kulturanalys av mejeridiskens nya ekonomi*. Höör: Brutus Östlings Bokförlag.

Kim, B. F., Santo, R. E., Scatterday, A. P., Fry, J. P., Synk, C. M., Cebron, S. R., Mehonnen, M. M., Hoekstra, A. Y., de Pee, S., Bloem, M. W., Neff, R. A., and Nachman, K. E., 2019. Country-specific dietary shifts to mitigate climate and water crises. *Global Environmental Change*, 62, 101926. http://doi.org/10.1016/j.gloenvcha.2019.05.010

Koning Beals, R., 2018. Is a lab-grown hamburger what's for dinner? *MarketWatch*. www.marketwatch.com/story/is-a-lab-grown-hamburger-whats-for-dinner-2018-02-21

Kurlansky, M., 2016. *Paper: Paging through History*. New York: W. W. Norton.

Leahy, E., Lyons, S., and Tol, R. S. J., 2010. An estimate of the number of vegetarians in the world. Working Paper No. 340. Economic and Social Research Institute (ESRI), Dublin. https://www.econstor.eu/bitstream/10419/50160/1/632222107.pdf

Lindmark, M., Bergquist, A. K., and Andersson, L. F., 2011. Energy transition, carbon dioxide reduction and output growth in the Swedish pulp and paper industry, 1973–2006. *Energy Policy*, 39(9), 5449–56.

Manning, J., 2019. Collapse at Oregon State University project trouble for CLT industry. *The Oregonian*. https://eu.statesmanjournal.com/story/news/2018/08/13/collapse-oregon-state-project-trouble-clt-industry/981611002/

Marchetti, C., 1977. On geoengineering and the CO_2 problem. *Climatic Change*, 1, 59–68.

Material Economics, 2019. Industrial transformation 2050 – Pathways to net-zero emissions from EU heavy industry. Material Economics, Stockholm. https://materialeconomics.com/material-economics-industrial-transformation-2050.pdf?cms_fileid=303ee49891120acc9ea3d13bbd498d13

Metcalfe, J., 2016. The winners of the C40 cities awards for climate change. Blomberg CityLab. www.bloomberg.com/news/articles/2016-12-02/the-winners-of-the-c40-cities-awards-for-climate-change

Metsä Fibre, n.d. Äänekoski bioproduct mill. www.metsafibre.com/en/about-us/Production-units/Bioproduct-mill/Pages/default.aspx#

Milford, R. L., Pauliuk, S., Allwood, J. M., and Müller, D. B., 2013. The roles of energy and material efficiency in meeting steel industry CO_2 targets. *Environmental Science & Technology*, 47, 3455–62.

Ministry of the Environment and Energy, 2018. The Swedish climate policy framework. www.government.se/information-material/2018/03/the-swedish-climate-policy-framework/

Mitchell, T., 2011. *Carbon Democracy: Political Power in the Age of Oil*. London: Verso.

Monforti-Ferrario, F., Dallemand, J.-F., Pinedo Pascua, I., Motola, V., Banja, M., Scarlat, N., Medarac, H., Castellazzi, L., Labanca, N., Bertoldi, P., Pennington, D., Goralczyk, M., Schau, E. M., Saouter, E., Sala, S., Notarnicola, B., Tassielli, G., and Renzulli, P., 2015. Energy use and the EU food sector: State of play and opportunities for improvement. European Commission, Joint Research Centre (JRC), Luxembourg. https://publications.jrc.ec.europa.eu/repository/bitstream/JRC96121/ldna27247enn.pdf

Mouat, M. J. and Prince, R., 2018. Cultured meat and cowless milk: On making markets for animal-free food. *Journal of Cultural Economy*, 11(4), 315–29. http://doi.org/10.1080/17530350.2018.1452277

Moya, J. A. and Pavel, C. C., 2018. Energy efficiency and GHG emissions: Prospective scenarios for the pulp and paper industry. EUR 29280 EN. Publications Office of the European Union, Luxembourg.

Mullendore, W. C. and Lutz, R. H., 1941. *History of the United States Food Administration 1917–1919*. Redwood City: Stanford University Press.

Mylan, J., Morris, C., Beech, E., and Geels, F. W., 2019. Rage against the regime: Niche-regime interactions in the societal embedding of plant-based milk. *Environmental Innovation and Societal Transitions*, 31, 233–47. www .sciencedirect.com/science/article/pii/S2210422418300066#bib0420

NFU, 2019. Achieving net zero: Farming's 2040 goal. National Farmers' Union (NFU). www.nfuonline.com/nfu-online/business/regulation/achieving-net-zero-farmings-2040-goal/

Nielsen, T. D., Hasselbalch, J., Holmberg, K., and Stripple, J., 2020. Politics and the plastic crisis: A review throughout the plastic life cycle. *Wiley Interdisciplinary Reviews: Energy and Environment*, 9(1), p. e360.

Nielsen, T. D., Holmberg, K., and Stripple, J., 2019. Need a bag? A review of public policies on plastic carrier bags – Where, how and to what effect? *Waste Management*, 87, 428–40.

Nilsson, M., Jordan, A., Turnpenny, J., Hertin, J., Nykvist, B., and Russel, D., 2008. The use and non-use of policy appraisal tools in public policy making: An analysis of three European countries and the European Union. *Policy Sciences*, 41, 335–55.

Novotny, M. and Nuur, C., 2013. The transformation of pulp and paper industries: The role of local networks and institutions. *International Journal of Innovation and Regional Development*, 5(1), 41–57.

OECD, 2018. Dairy and dairy products. OECD-FAO Agricultural Outlook 2018–2027. Organisation for Economic Co-operation and Development (OECD), Paris. www.agri-outlook.org/commodities/Agricultural-Outlook-2018-Dairy.pdf

OECD, 2020. Latest developments in steelmaking capacity. Organisation for Economic Co-operation and Development (OECD), Paris.

OECD and FAO, 2016. OECD/FAO agricultural outlook 2016–2025. Organisation for Economic Co-operation and Development (OECD), Paris. http://doi.org/10.1787/agr_outlook-2016-10-en

Pardo, N., Moya, J. A., and Vatopoulos, K., 2012. Prospective scenarios on energy efficiency and CO_2 emissions in the EU iron & steel industry. Publications Office of the European Union, Luxembourg.

Pauliuk, S., Milford, R. L., Muller, D. B., and Allwod, J. M., 2013. The steel scrap age. *Environmental Science Technology*, 47, 3448–54. http://doi.org/10.1021/es303149z

Pe'er, G., Lakner, S., Müller, R., Passoni, G., Bontzorlos, V., Clough, D., Moreira, F., Azam, C., Berger, J., Bezak, P., Bonn, A., Hansjürgens, B., Hartmann, L., Kleemann, J., Lomba, A., Sahrbacher, A., Schindler, S., Schleyer, C., Schmidt, J., Schüler, S., Sirami, C., von Meyer-Höfer, M., and Zinngrebe, Y., 2017. *Is the CAP Fit for Purpose? An Evidence-Based Fitness-Check Assessment.* Leipzig: German Centre for Integrative Biodiversity Research.

Pe'er, G., Zinngrebe, Y., Moreira, F., Sirami, C., Schindler, S., Müller, R., Bontzorlos, V., Clough, D., Bezák, P., Bonn, A., Hansjürgens, B., Lomba, A., Möckel, S., Passoni, G., Schleyer, C., Schmidt, J., and Lakner, S., 2019. A greener path for the EU common agricultural policy. *Science*, 365(6452), 449–51.

PlasticsEurope, 2019. Plastics – The facts 2019: An analysis of European plastics production, demand and waste data. PlasticsEurope, Brussels. https://plasticseurope.org/wp-content/uploads/2021/10/2019-Plastics-the-facts.pdf

Pohjanmies, T., Triviño, M., Le Tortorec, E., Salminen, H., and Mönkkönen, M., 2017. Conflicting objectives in production forests pose a challenge for forest management. *Ecosystem Services*, 28, 298–310. http://doi.org/10.1016/j.ecoser.2017.06.018

Poore, J. and Nemecek, T., 2018. Reducing food's environmental impacts through producers and consumers. *Science*, 360(6392), 987–92.

Quader, M. A., Ahmed, S., Dawal, S. Z., and Nukman, Y., 2016. Present needs, recent progress and future trends of energy-efficient ultra-low carbon dioxide (CO_2) steelmaking (ULCOS) program. *Renewable and Sustainable Energy Reviews*, 55, 527–49. http://doi.org/10.1016/j.rser.2015.10.101

Research and Markets, 2021. Cultured meat market – A global market and regional analysis: Focus on cultured meat product and application, investment analysis, and country analysis – Analysis and forecast, 2026–2030. Report ID: 5237661.

Ritchie, H. and Roser, M., 2017. Meat and dairy production. *Our World in Data*. https://ourworldindata.org/meat-production#per-capita-milk-consumption

Ritchie, H. and Roser, M., 2019. Meat and dairy production. *Our World in Data*. https://ourworldindata.org/meat-production

Rothgerber, H., 2013. Real men don't eat (vegetable) quiche: Masculinity and the justification of meat consumption. *Psychology of Men & Masculinity*, 14, 363–75.

Sandberg, M., 2021. Sufficiency transitions: A review of consumption changes for environmental sustainability. *Journal of Cleaner Production*, 293, 126097. http://doi.org/10.1016/j.jclepro.2021.126097

Santos, D. and Lane, R., 2017. A material lens on socio-technical transitions: The case of steel in Australian buildings. *Geoforum*, 82, 40–50. http://doi.org/10.1016/j.geoforum.2017.03.020

Scarborough, P. and Rayner, M., 2010. Nutrient density to climate impact index is an inappropriate system for ranking beverages in order of climate impact per nutritional value. *Food & Nutrition Research*, 54, 5681. http://doi.org/10.3402/fnr.v54i0.5681

Schebesta, H. and Candel, J. J. L., 2020. Game-changing potential of the EU's farm to fork strategy. *Nature Food*, 1, 586–8. http://doi.org/10.1038/s43016-020-00166-9

Schösler, H., de Boer, J., and Boersma, J. J., 2012. Can we cut out the meat of the dish? Constructing consumer-oriented pathways towards meat substitution. *Appetite*, 58, 39–47.

Seto, K. C., Davis, S. J., Mitchell, R. B., Stokes, E. C., Unruh, G., and Ürge-Vorsatz, D., 2016. Carbon lock-in: Types, causes, and policy implications. *Annual Review of Environment and Resources*, 41, 425–52. http://doi.org/10.1146/annurev-environ-110615-085934

Sexton, A. E., Garnett, T., and Lorimer, J., 2019. Framing the future of food: The contested promises of alternative proteins. *Environment and Planning E: Nature and Space*, 2(1), 47–72.

Sharma, S., 2020. Milking the planet. Institute for Agriculture & Trade Policy, Minneapolis. www.iatp.org/milking-planet

Smedman, A., 2017. Mjölk är 8 gånger bättre än havredryck. www.mjolk.se/artiklar/mjolk-ar-8-ganger-battre-an-havredryck/#!/artiklar/mjolk-ar-8-ganger-battre-an-havredryck/

Smink, M. M., Hekkert, M., and Negro, S., 2015. Keeping sustainable innovation on a leash? Exploring incumbents' institutional strategies. *Business Strategy and the Environment*, 24(2), 86–101.

Smith, A. and Raven, R., 2012. What is protective space? Reconsidering niches in transitions to sustainability. *Research Policy*, 41, 1025–36. http://doi.org/10.1016/j.respol.2011.12.012

Stehfest, E., van Vuuren, D. P., Kram, T., Bouwman, L., Alkemade, R., Bakkenes, M., Biemans, H., Bouwman, A., den Elzen, M. G. J., Janse, J., Lucas, P., Van Minnen, J., Müller, C., and Prins, A., 2014. Integrated assessment of global environmental change with IMAGE 3.0: Model description and policy applications. PBL Netherlands Environmental Assessment Agency, The Hague. www.pbl.nl/en/publications/integrated-assessment-of-global-environmental-change-with-IMAGE-3.0

Stephens, N., Sexton, A. E., and Driessen, C., 2019. Making sense of making meat: Key moments in the first 20 years of tissue engineering muscle to make food. *Frontiers in Sustainable Food Systems*, 3. http://doi.org/10.3389/fsufs.2019.00045

Stripple, J. and Bulkeley, H., 2019. Towards a material politics of sociotechnical transitions: Navigating decarbonisation pathways in Malmö. *Political Geography*, 72, 52–63.

Söderholm, P. and Lundmark, R., 2009. The development of forest-based biorefineries: Implications for market behavior and policy. *Forest Products Journal*, 59(1/2), 6–16.

Tatum, M., 2020. Spilt milk: Covid-19 and dairy. *Wicked Leeks*. https://wickedleeks.riverford.co.uk/features/dairy-farming-price/spilt-milk-covid-19-and-dairy

The Climate Change Act 2008 (2050 Target Amendment) Order 2019, 2019. www.legislation.gov.uk/ukpga/2008/27/contents

The Climate Group, 2021. Steel zero. www.theclimategroup.org/steelzero

The Tissue Culture and Art Project, 2021. Disembodied Cuisine. https://tcaproject.net/portfolio/disembodied-cuisine/

The Vegan Society, 2019. Statistics. www.vegansociety.com/news/media/statistics

ThyssenKrupp, 2019. Press release: Thyssenkrupp sets clear targets: Group aims to be climate neutral by 2050 – 30 percent emissions reduction planned for 2030. www.thyssenkrupp.com/en/newsroom/press-releases/thyssenkrupp-sets-clear-targets–group-aims-to-be-climate-neutral-by-2050—30-per cent-emissions-reduction-planned-for-2030-12803.html

Tziva, M., Negro, S., Kalfagianni, A., and Hekkert, M. P., 2020. Understanding the protein transition: The rise of plant-based meat substitutes. *Environmental Innovation and Societal Transitions*, 35, 217–31.

Tönjes, A., Mölter, H., Pastowski, A., and Witte, K., 2019. Summary of decarbonisation case studies. Project Deliverable 3.3, H2020 REINVENT Project Nr 730053. https://static1.squarespace.com/static/59f0cb986957da5faf64971e/t/5d23b2550832210001a02b65/1562620507471/D3.3+Summary+of+Decarbonisation+Case+Studies.pdf

UNEP, 2016. Annual report 2016. United Nations Environment Programme (UNEP), Nairobi. https://www.unep.org/annualreport/2016/index.php

UNFCCC, 2015. Adoption of the Paris Agreement. FCCC/CP/2015/L.9/Rev.1. United Nations Framework Convention on Climate Change (UNFCCC), Bonn.

Unruh, G. C., 2000. Understanding carbon lock-in. *Energy Policy*, 28, 817–30.

Valenze, D., 2011. *Milk: A Local and Global History*. London: Yale University Press.

Van Ruijven, B. J., Van Vuuren, D. P., Boskaljon, W., Neelis, M. L., Saygin, D., and Patel, M. K., 2016. Long-term model-based projections of energy use and CO_2 emissions from the global steel and cement industries. *Resources, Conservation and Recycling*, 112, 15–36.

Van Sluisveld, M. A. E., De Boer, H. S., Daioglou, V., Hof, A. F., and van Vuuren, D. P., 2020. Deliverable D4.10 – Assessing the cumulative impacts of sectoral decarbonisation pathways for heavy industry. Project Deliverable 4.10, H2020 REINVENT Project Nr 730053. https://static1 .squarespace.com/static/59f0cb986957da5faf64971e/t/5f7dae2783c0fd5b6 fe96b46/1602072113459/D4.10+Assessing+the+cumulative+impacts+of +sectoral+decarbonisation+pathways+for+heavy+industry%28updated% 29.pdf

Van Sluisveld, M. A. E., De Boer, H. S., Hof, A. F., van Vuuren, D. P., Schneider, C., and Lechtenboehmer, S., 2018. EU decarbonisation scenarios for industry. Project Deliverable 4.2, H2020 REINVENT Project Nr 730053. https://static1.squarespace.com/static/59f0cb986957da5faf64971e/t/ 5b3fdf266d2a73e319355e0c/1530912585721/D4.2+EU+decarbonisation +scenarios+for+industry.pdf

VDP, 2019. Facts about paper. Verband Deutscher Papierfabriken (VDP), Bonn.

Voinov, A. and Bousquet, F., 2010. Modelling with stakeholders. *Environmental Modelling & Software*, 25(11), 1268–81. http://doi.org/ 10.1016/j.envsoft.2010.03.007

Watts, G., 2019. The cows that could help fight climate change. *BBC Future*. www.bbc.com/future/article/20190806-how-vaccines-could-fix-our-prob lem-with-cow-emissions

Weis, T., 2015. Meatification and the madness of the double narrative. *Canadian Food Studies*, 2(2), 296–303.

Wesseling, J. H., Lechtenböhmer, S., Åhman, M., Nilsson, L. J., Worrell, E., and Coenen, L., 2017. The transition of energy intensive processing industries towards deep decarbonization: Characteristics and implications for future research. *Renewable and Sustainable Energy Reviews*, 79, 1303–13.

Wild, F., Czerny, M., Janssen, A. M., Kole, A. P. W., Zunabovic, M., and Domig, K. J., 2014. The evolution of a plant-based alternative to meat: From niche markets to widely accepted meat alternatives. *Sustainability*, 25 (1), 45-49.

Willett, W., Rockström, J., Loken, B., Springmann, M., Lang, T., Vermeulen, S., Garnett, T., Tilman, D., DeClerck, F., Wood, A., Jonell, M, Clark, M., Gordon, L. J., Fanzo, J., Hawkes, C., Zurayk, R., Rivera, J. A., De Vries, W., Majele Sibanda, L., Afshin, A., Chaudhary, A., Herrero, M., Augustina, R., Branca, F., Lartey, A., Fan, S., Crona, B., Fox, E.,

Bignet, V., Troell, M., Lindahl, T., Singh, S., Cornell, S. E., Srinath Reddy, K., Narain, S., Nishtar, S. , and Murray, C. J. L., 2019. Food in the Anthropocene: The EAT–*Lancet* Commission on healthy diets from sustainable food systems. *Lancet*, 393, 447–92. http://doi.org/10.1016/S0140-6736(18)31788-4

Wolf, M. J. P, 2012. *Building Imaginary Worlds: The Theory and History of Subcreation*. New York: Routledge.

Wood, T., Dundas, G., and Ha, J., 2020. Start with steel. Report No. 2020-06. Grattan Institute, Melbourne. ISBN: 978-0-6487380-6-0

World Steel Association, 2020. Oor Materiality Assessment. https://www.world steel.org/steel-by-topic/sustainability/sustainability-commitment/material ity-assessment.html

WSP Parsons Brinckerhoff and DNV GL, 2015a. Industrial decarbonisation & energy efficiency roadmaps to 2050 – Food and drink. https://assets.publish ing.service.gov.uk/government/uploads/system/uploads/attachment_data/ file/416672/Food_and_Drink_Report.pdf

WSP Parsons Brinckerhoff and DNV GL, 2015b. Industrial decarbonisation & energy efficiency roadmaps to 2050 – Iron and steel. https://assets.publish ing.service.gov.uk/government/uploads/system/uploads/attachment_data/ file/416667/Iron_and_Steel_Report.pdf

WSP Parsons Brinckerhoff and DNV GL, 2015c. Industrial decarbonisation & energy efficiency roadmaps to 2050 – Pulp and paper. https://assets.publish ing.service.gov.uk/government/uploads/system/uploads/attachment_data/ file/416673/Pulp_and_Paper_Report.pdf

Yates, L., 2015. Rethinking prefiguration: Alternatives, micropolitics and goals in social movements. *Social Movement Studies*, 14(1), 1–21.

Zero Waste Europe, 2017. Seizing the opportunity: Using plastic only where it makes sense. Zero Waste Europe, Brussels. https://zerowasteeurope.eu/wp-content/uploads/2019/11/zero_waste_europe_position_paper_plastics_re duction_targets_en.pdf

Acknowledgements

The authors would like to thank all colleagues in the REINVENT project (2016–2020). Without the collective efforts and our joint learning about decarbonisation across value chains this Element would not have been possible. We also thank the range of stakeholders from industry, NGOs, government, and other organisations who participated in the many workshops and other events. REINVENT was funded by the European Commission under H2020 contract no. 730053.

About the Authors

Harriet Bulkeley FBA FAcSS holds joint appointments as Professor in the Department of Geography, Durham University, and at the Copernicus Institute of Sustainable Development, Utrecht University. Her research focuses on environmental governance and the politics of climate change, energy, and sustainable cities. She has published eight books, several edited collections and over 60 papers, including *An Urban Politics of Climate Change* (Routledge 2015) and *Accomplishing Climate Governance* (CUP 2016).

Johannes Stripple researches climate change and its governance through a range of sites, from the insurance industry, the petrochemical industry to carbon markets, from the UN to the urban and the everyday. He has edited *Governing the Climate: New Approaches to Rationality, Power and Politics* (CUP 2014) and *Towards a Cultural Politics of Climate Change* (CUP 2016).

Lars J. Nilsson has 30 years of experience in the fields of energy and environmental systems studies, technology assessments, and policy analysis. Recent research is on low-carbon transition strategies, policy, and governance in the energy- and emission-intensive industry. He teaches on energy and climate science and politics at Lund University.

Bregje van Veelen is a social researcher with an interest in the governance of low-carbon transitions. Her research explores lowcarbon governance at different scales, the socio-material dynamics of carbon lock-in, and the potential for low-carbon transitions to contribute to societal transformation and political democratisation.

Agni Kalfagianni specialises in the effectiveness, legitimacy, and ethical and justice considerations of private and transnational forms of governance in the sustainability domain. Her work has appeared in numerous international peer-reviewed journals and edited volumes with major university presses.

Fredric Bauer holds a PhD from Lund University, where he is now a researcher focused on the development and diffusion of low-carbon innovation in energy- and emissions-intensive industries as well as institutional change for socio-technical transitions towards sustainability.

Mariësse van Sluisveld is a climate policy researcher at Lund University with extensive knowledge of quantitative scenarios and metrics on systems change along the Paris Climate Agreement. Previously, she held positions as a climate policy researcher at PBL Netherlands Environmental Assessment Agency and Utrecht University in the Netherlands.

Cambridge Elements ☰

Earth System Governance

Frank Biermann
Utrecht University

Frank Biermann is Research Professor of Global Sustainability Governance with the Copernicus Institute of Sustainable Development, Utrecht University, the Netherlands. He is the founding Chair of the Earth System Governance Project, a global transdisciplinary research network launched in 2009; and Editor-in-Chief of the new peer-reviewed journal *Earth System Governance* (Elsevier). In April 2018, he won a European Research Council Advanced Grant for a research program on the steering effects of the Sustainable Development Goals.

Aarti Gupta
Wageningen University

Aarti Gupta is Professor of Global Environmental Governance at Wageningen University, The Netherlands. She is Lead Faculty and a member of the Scientific Steering Committee of the Earth System Governance (ESG) Project and a Coordinating Lead Author of its 2018 Science and Implementation Plan. She is also principal investigator of the Dutch Research Council-funded TRANSGOV project on the Transformative Potential of Transparency in Climate Governance. She holds a PhD from Yale University in environmental studies.

About the Series

Linked with the Earth System Governance Project, this exciting new series will provide concise but authoritative studies of the governance of complex socio-ecological systems, written by world-leading scholars. Highly interdisciplinary in scope, the series will address governance processes and institutions at all levels of decision-making, from local to global, within a planetary perspective that seeks to align current institutions and governance systems with the fundamental 21st Century challenges of global environmental change and earth system transformations.

Elements in this series will present cutting edge scientific research, while also seeking to contribute innovative transformative ideas towards better governance. A key aim of the series is to present policy-relevant research that is of interest to both academics and policy-makers working on earth system governance.

More information about the Earth System Governance project can be found at: www.earthsystemgovernance.org.

Earth System Governance